Disclaimer

CCPs provide long term guidance for management decisions and set forth goals, objectives, and strategies needed to accomplish refuge purposes and identify the Service's best estimate of future needs. These plans detail program planning levels that are sometimes substantially above current budget allocations and, as such, are primarily for Service strategic planning and program prioritization purposes. The plans do not constitute a commitment for staffing increases, operational and maintenance increases, or funding for future land acquisition.

San Joaquin River
National Wildlife Refuge

Draft Comprehensive Conservation Plan

Prepared by:
U.S. Fish and Wildlife Service
California/Nevada Operations Office

San Luis National Wildlife Refuge Complex
947-C West Pacheco Blvd.
Los Banos, CA 93635

California/Nevada Refuge Planning Office
2800 Cottage Way, W-1832
Sacramento, CA 95825

Approved by: _____ **Date**_____
California/Nevada Operations Manager

Contents

Figures

Tables

Appendices 89

1 Introduction

This Comprehensive Conservation Plan (CCP) will guide the management of the San Joaquin River National Wildlife Refuge (NWR) for the next 15 years. The San Joaquin River NWR is one of over 500 refuges that comprise the U.S. Fish and Wildlife Service's National Wildlife Refuge System. The mission of the National Wildlife Refuge System is to conserve a network of lands and water for the conservation and management of fish, wildlife and plant resources of the United States for the benefit of present and future generations. As part of the system, the San Joaquin River NWR provides a haven for a unique assemblage of both wetland and upland dependent wildlife species of California's Central Valley.

California's Central Valley is ecologically diverse and rich in wildlife. The Valley averages forty miles wide by four hundred miles long and consists of two lesser valleys (Sacramento in the north and San Joaquin in the south) and a delta where the two drainages meet. San Joaquin River NWR is located within the San Joaquin Valley, which is bounded by the Sacramento/San Joaquin Delta to the north, the Tehachapi Mountains to the south, the Sierra Nevada to the east and the Coast Range to the west. The San Joaquin Valley is divided into two distinct drainage basins; the San Joaquin basin in the northern two-thirds, where the Refuge is located, and the Tulare basin in the southern one-third. The San Joaquin River and its tributaries drain the San Joaquin Basin.

Historically, the Central Valley was a vast grassland that graded up the sides of the foothills of the surrounding mountains. The grasslands were once dominated by perennial bunchgrasses, which provided rich forage for numerous grazers, including pronghorn antelope (*Antilocapra americana*), elk (*Cervus elaphus nannodes*) and mule deer (*Odocoileus hemionus*), and a complex suite of small grazers and seed predators *(Barbour and Billings 1988)*. They also supported an array of grassland-dependent birds, including songbirds, birds of prey and gamebirds. Woodlands meandered across these grasslands in belts that varied from half a mile to six miles wide along rivers. Oak woodlands, which had a park-like quality, became more dense and mixed with cottonwoods (*Populus* spp.), sycamores (*Plantanus* spp.), ash (*Fraxinus* spp.) and willow (*Salix* spp.) near the river edges and sloughs *(Barbour and Billings 1988)*. Acorns produced by valley oaks (*Quercus lobata*) and other oaks (*Quercus* spp.) provided abundant forage for numerous wildlife species *(Bonnicksen 2000, McShea and Healy 2002)*. The riparian tracts and woodlands served as forested habitat for diverse breeding and migratory songbirds, provided nesting sites for birds of prey and colonial nesting waterbirds, and acted as travel corridors for forest-dependent wildlife. Extensive marshes were a dominant feature along the water courses of the valley, some large enough to be almost impassable *(Ornduff 1974)*. The marshes were dominated by monocots particularly tules (*Scirpus* spp.), cattails (*Typha* spp.) and sedges (*Carex* spp. and *Cyperus* spp.). These wetlands hosted one of the largest concentrations of wintering waterfowl in the world. In the mid-1800s, early explorers reported vast numbers of waterfowl and other marsh and shorebirds in the Central Valley.

During the last 150 years, the natural resources of the Central Valley have been severely altered with the increase in cultivation, ranching, urban centers and industry. These changes significantly altered or reduced a majority of the valley's native habitats and ecological processes. The former native, perennial grasslands that once dominated the valley are now composed of "weedy," non-native annual grasses, such as *Avena, Bromus, Lolium* and *Erodium* species, plus a large number of non-native forbs *(Barbour and Billings 1988)*. Large, herbivorous wildlife are no longer dominant or, in some cases, present. The once-stately valley oak woodlands, which formerly supported the largest oaks in North America, have been decimated with the changing land use. Much of the riparian forest along stream and river corridors has also been eliminated *(Bonnicksen 2000)*. Of the eight oak woodland types of the Pacific Coast, the valley oak woodland is now the second rarest by total acreage *(McShea and Healy 2002)*. Suppression efforts and changing land use have reduced fire as a natural process within much of the Central Valley; both water demands and flood control activities for urban centers and agriculture have drastically transformed the natural hydrology. As a result, these changes have destroyed or modified over 95 percent of the historic wetlands in California *(Heitmeyer et al. 1989)*.

Although the Central Valley has been altered since settlement, it still supports nationally important and critical natural resources. During the 1970s, an estimated ten to twelve million ducks, geese and swans wintered in, or migrated through, California *(Heitmeyer et al. 1989)*. California wetlands occur primarily in the Central Valley, as do most waterfowl. No other area in North America is as important for wintering waterfowl as California. California supports greater than 60 percent of all waterfowl (excluding sea ducks) wintering in the Pacific Flyway and about 20 percent in the entire United States. The Central Valley plays the most significant role in California's importance to waterfowl. San Joaquin River NWR supports significant waterfowl and waterbird resources and

is capable of providing habitat for an even greater abundance of these trust resources. The Refuge has the potential for protecting and restoring many of the unique, native upland and wetland habitats of the Central Valley and the wildlife which they support.

Background

San Joaquin River NWR was established in 1987 to primarily protect and manage wintering habitat for Aleutian Canada geese[1] *(Branta canadensis leucopareia)*, a federally listed endangered species. Since that time, the Refuge's focus has expanded to include other threatened and endangered species, migratory birds, wildlife dependent on wetlands and riparian floodplain habitat, and restoration of habitat and ecological processes. Nonetheless, providing wintering habitat for and protecting Aleutian Canada geese has remained a primary objective of the Refuge since its beginning. This Refuge and its management have been important factors in the recovery of the Aleutian Canada goose and its removal in 2001 from the Threatened and Endangered Species List.

The Aleutian Canada goose is a small Canada goose subspecies; its size is between the cackling Canada goose (smallest subspecies) and Taverner's Canada goose *(Johnson et al. 1979)*. The historic breeding grounds for the Aleutian are believed to have extended from near Kodiak Island, Alaska, to the Kuril Islands in Asia. Their wintering grounds included Japan, and North America, from British Columbia to northern Mexico *(Delecour 1954)*. The population declined during the early 1900s due to the introduction of Arctic *(Alopex lagopus)* and red *(Vulpes vulpes)* foxes to their nesting islands. At the time of listing (1975), the population was estimated at 800 individuals. The species was delisted in 2001 and the population now numbers over 40,000 individuals *(Fitzmorris 2002)*. At present,

---

[1] Subsequent to preparation of this plan, the American Ornithological Union made major revisions to the taxonomy of Canada geese (Banks et al. 2003). Aleutian Canada geese are now classified as Aleutian cackling geese *(Branta hutchinsii leucopariea)*. For purposes of this document the old classification (Aleutian Canada goose) will be used in the text.

San Joaquin River NWR and adjacent lands are the primary wintering grounds for the Aleutian Canada goose population.

The Refuge is part of the San Luis NWR Complex, which includes three other units: Merced NWR, San Luis NWR and the Grassland Wildlife Management Area. All four of the Refuge units, including the San Joaquin River NWR, are managed by the Complex.

Purpose and Need for a Plan

The U.S. Fish and Wildlife Service (Service) is developing comprehensive conservation plans (CCP) to guide the management and resource use for each refuge of the National Wildlife Refuge System (Refuge System). The Refuge System includes over 500 individual Refuges, forming the largest network of public lands in the world managed principally for fish and wildlife.

A CCP provides a description of the desired future conditions and long-range guidance necessary for meeting refuge purposes. The CCP and associated environmental assessment (EA) meet the mandates of the National Wildlife Refuge Improvement Act of 1977 (Improvement Act) and address Service mandates, policies, goals and appropriate National Environmental Policy Act (NEPA) compliance. The Service's future management plan for the San Joaquin River NWR is provided in this document. The final plan is developed according to revisions made during internal and public review.

Refuge staff will use this CCP as a management tool. The CCP will guide management decisions for the next 15 years and sets forth strategies for achieving Refuge goals and objectives within that time frame.

The Refuge does not currently have a comprehensive management plan that provides guidance for managing habitat, wildlife and public use. The intent of the CCP is to describe how the Refuge's founding purposes should be pursued over the next 15 years. The plan sets Refuge goals and objectives and provides strategies for achieving them based on specific Refuge purposes, Federal laws, National Wildlife Refuge System goals and Service policies. Management activities are selected based on their efficacy in fulfilling Refuge goals and objectives.

The CCP is comprehensive as it addresses all activities that occur on the Refuge; however, the noted management activities or strategies are broadly stated. The Refuge staff will prepare detailed step-down plans that follow the CCP process and describe how a management strategy, such as developing an interpretive program, will be applied. These plans are adjusted based on monitoring results, available funds, staff and current Service policy. The effects of management actions are monitored to provide information for needed modifications of management practices or activities. The CCP has flexibility and will be reviewed periodically to ensure that its goals, objectives, strategies and time frames remain valid.

The Service is preparing this plan for the Refuge to:

■ Provide a basis for management that is consistent with the Refuge System mission and Refuge purposes and ensure that the needs of wildlife come first, before other uses.

■ Provide a scientific foundation for Refuge management.

■ Provide a clear vision statement of the desired future conditions when Refuge purposes and goals have been accomplished.

■ Provide visitors with a clear understanding of the reasons for management actions on the Refuge.

■ Ensure the compatibility of current and future uses of the Refuge.

■ Provide long-term continuity in Refuge management.

■ Provide a basis for operation, maintenance and development budget requests.

The CCP will guide management decisions for the next 15 years.

San Joaquin River National Wildlife Refuge will be managed to conserve, protect and enhance native communities of the San Joaquin Valley.

Refuge Purpose and Authority

The Refuge was established in 1987 to provide winter forage and roosting habitat for the threatened Aleutian Canada goose, protect other species federally listed as endangered/threatened, improve and manage habitat for migratory birds and conserve native fauna and flora. The Service established the Refuge as a unit of the San Luis NWR Complex under authority of the Endangered Species Act of 1973, Migratory Bird Conservation Act of 1929 and the Fish and Wildlife Act of 1956.

The Refuge purposes as stated in the law are:

"To conserve fish or wildlife which are listed as endangered species or threatened species or plants..." 16 U.S.C. § 1534 (Endangered Species Act of 1973);

"...For use as an inviolate sanctuary, or for any other management purpose, for migratory birds." 16 U.S.C. § 715d (Migratory Bird Conservation Act); and

"...For the development, advancement, management, conservation, and protection of fish and wildlife resources." 16 U.S.C. § 742f(a)(4) "...for the benefit of the United States Fish and Wildlife Service, in performing its activities and services. Such acceptance may be subject to the terms of any restrictive or affirmative covenant, or condition and servitude." 16 U.S.C. § 742f(b)(1) (Fish and Wildlife Act of 1956).

Refuge Vision Statement

San Joaquin River National Wildlife Refuge will be managed to conserve, protect and enhance native communities of the San Joaquin Valley, with a focus on wildlife and the ecological processes on which they depend. A large segment of the native valley habitats and their associated wildlife communities have been reduced due to intensive land use and development. This Refuge will conserve and restore the area's native habitats, maintaining its role as an important riparian corridor for natural resources within the state's Central Valley. It will emphasize management of native wildlife and the necessary actions that focus on the recovery of Federal and State listed endangered/threatened species and other species of special concern, and protection and/or enhancement of migratory bird resources. Waterfowl and other waterbirds, in particular the Aleutian Canada goose, and neotropical migratory birds, are management priorities. The San Joaquin River NWR will be a key link—along with other National Wildlife Refuges in the Pacific Flyway—in providing high quality, native habitat, particularly wetlands that support an abundance and diversity of waterbirds.

The Refuge will support a variety of native habitats, ranging from valley oak gallery and mixed riparian forests/woodlands to seasonal and permanent wetlands, from native grasslands to modified habitats, in order to support and benefit select trust wildlife species, particularly those of special concern. These habitats will support a wide diversity of native fish, wildlife and plants, such as anadromous fish, neotropical migratory birds, waterfowl and other waterbirds, as well as resident wildlife.

The Refuge will provide an ideal environment for environmental education about native California habitats/wildlife and their conservation/restoration. It will provide the public with excellent wildlife viewing and photographic opportunities, as well as traditional area activities, including waterfowl hunting and fishing.

Location and Size of the Refuge

The Refuge is nine miles west of the City of Modesto, California, and straddles western Stanislaus and San Joaquin counties. The Refuge is located in the northern portion of the San Joaquin Valley, which is enclosed by the foothills of the Sierra Nevada Mountains to the east and the Coast Range to the west. The other units of San Luis NWR Complex, San Luis and Merced NWRs are located approximately thirty-five and forty miles south, respectively, from San Joaquin River NWR. The 12,887 acres within the approved boundary of San Joaquin River NWR are along the main stem of the

San Joaquin River from just south of the confluence with the Tuolumne River, then north to the south bank of the Stanislaus River. The Mohler Tract of the Refuge is a noncontiguous parcel situated on the north bank of the Stanislaus River three miles east from the main portion of the Refuge. The Refuge's landscape represents a locally—as well as regionally—significant remnant of the once broad floodplain of these three major rivers of California's Central Valley (Figure 1–Watershed/ Ecosystem Map and Figure 2–Regional & Project Location Map). Surrounding lands are largely used in agricultural production.

Ownership

Lands within the Refuge boundary have been acquired in both fee title (outright purchases) and through easements (See Figure 3–Land Status Map). All acquisitions were on a willing-seller basis. Fee title lands are owned by the Service and serve as the core of Refuge lands. These lands are managed for wildlife as the priority.

Easement lands are privately-owned lands, where a willing owner has sold restricted land-use rights to the Service to protect or enhance wildlife habitats on these private lands. Typically, Service easement lands occur in proximity to fee title lands. The Service perpetual conservation easements were established to protect existing resource habitat values while retaining land in private ownership. In addition, the U.S. Department of Agriculture National Resource Conservation Service (NRCS) holds both Wetland Reserve Program and floodplain easements on some parcels of the Service-owned lands. The NRCS Wetland Reserve Program and floodplain easements were a funding partnership to acquire fee title land for the Service, whereby the NRCS purchased easements on the land and the Service paid the landowner the remaining fee title value. The land is then owned and managed in perpetuity by the Service with an underlying NRCS easement.

Refuge Acquisition History

The Service became interested in the present Refuge locale in 1976 when the federally-listed Aleutian Canada goose was discovered using the Faith Ranch and Mapes Ranch as winter habitat. At that time, the Faith Ranch was owned by the Paul Davies family and the Mapes Ranch by the Bill Lyons, Sr. family. Both ranches were primarily beef cattle operations, although the Mapes Ranch also had a small amount of row crop agricultural production. Although bounded by riparian habitat to the north, west and south, the uplands of both ranches were dominated by short-cropped irrigated pasture, scattered wetlands and stock ponds. This complex of habitats formed optimum foraging and roosting habitat for wintering Aleutian Canada geese. Subsequent monitoring revealed that more than 98 percent of the Aleutian Canada goose population wintered on these lands. The open terrain of the ranches provided high quality habitat for other geese, lesser and greater sandhill cranes, as well as other wildlife. The Service established the San Joaquin River NWR in 1987 for the primary purpose of meeting the wintering habitat objectives of the Aleutian Canada Goose Recovery Plan. At that time, the approved Refuge acquisition boundary (the area within which the Service could acquire and manage land) totaled 10,295 acres, and included primarily the Faith Ranch and Mapes Ranch east of the San Joaquin River, and a portion of another property west of the river. Initially, all Refuge land acquisition was planned as fee title purchase.

The first land acquisition occurred in 1988 when the Service purchased the 777 acre Christman Island from the National Audubon Society. Christman Island, formerly part of the Mapes Ranch, had been purchased by the Audubon Society in 1986 through a donation from Joseph M. Long and Don Lundberg, with the intent of reselling it the Service. During this time, the Service Realty Office was meeting with the Davies family landowners to pursue purchase of other lands within the acquisition boundary. For a variety

Figure 1: Watershed / Ecosystem Map

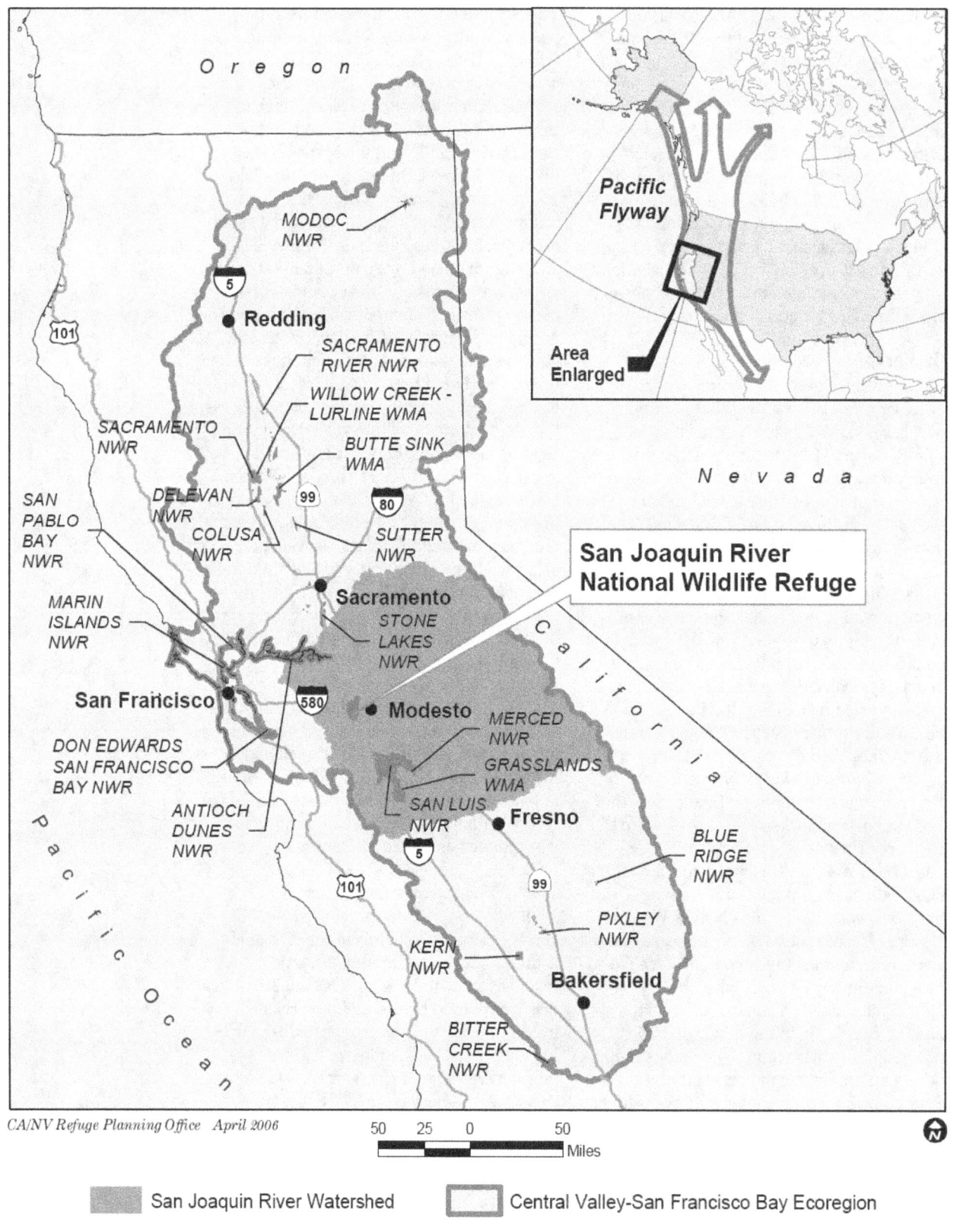

CA/NV Refuge Planning Office   April 2006

San Joaquin River Watershed   Central Valley-San Francisco Bay Ecoregion

Figure 2: Location Map

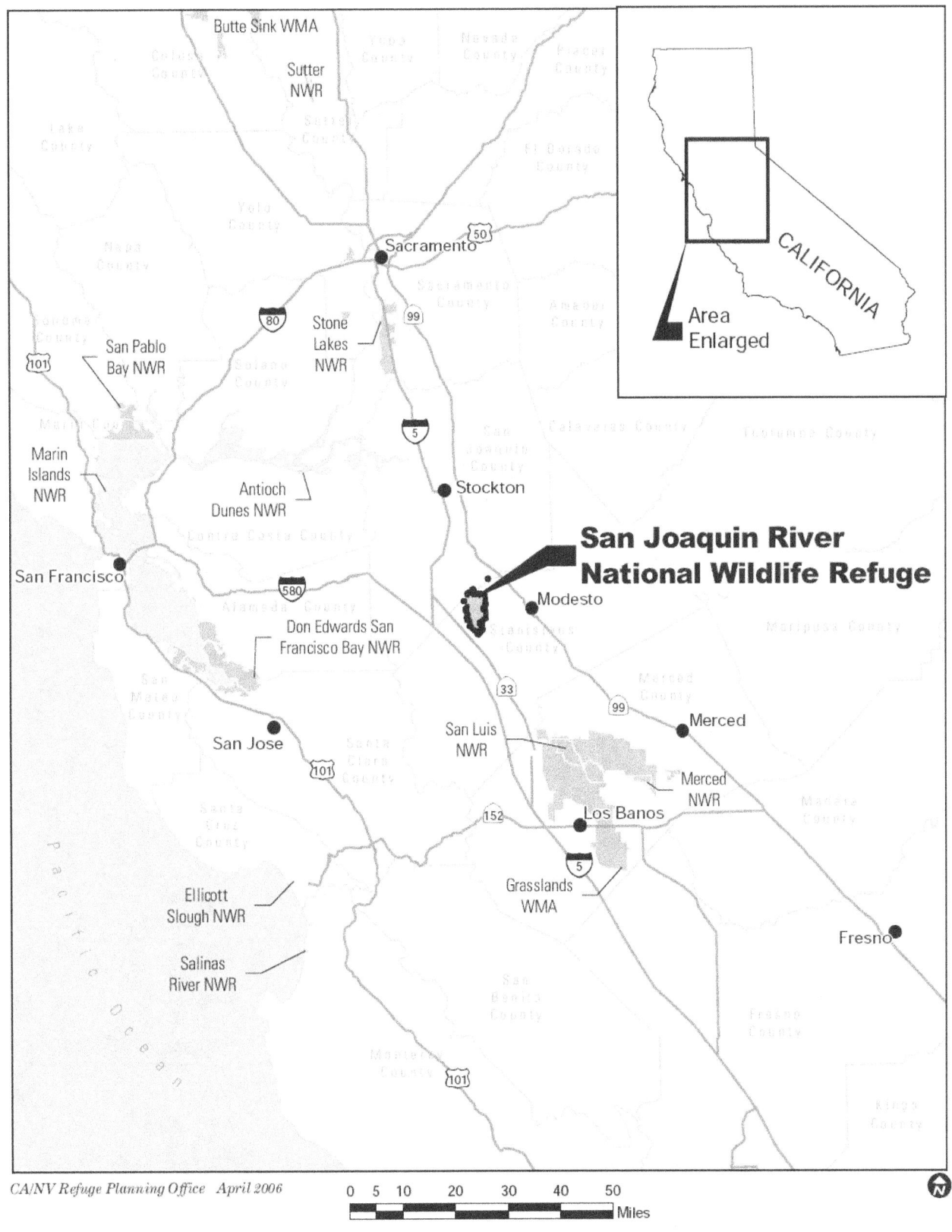

Figure 3: Land Status

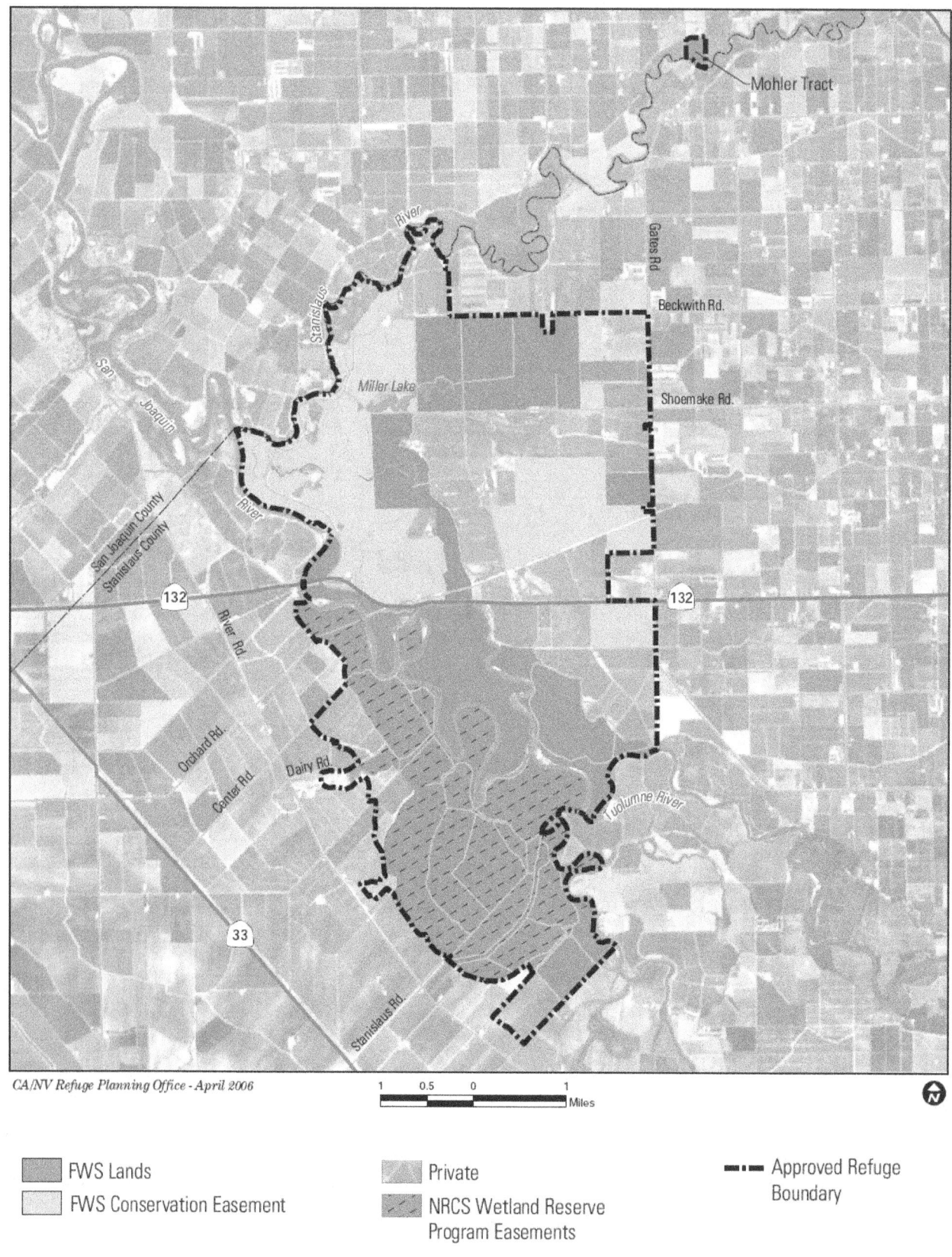

CA/NV Refuge Planning Office - April 2006

1   0.5   0   1
Miles

	FWS Lands			Private		Approved Refuge Boundary
	FWS Conservation Easement			NRCS Wetland Reserve Program Easements		

of reasons these negotiations were unsuccessful.

In 1990, the Robert Gallo family purchased the Faith Ranch. The new landowners were not interested in selling the ranch to the Service, but were willing to enroll the ranch in a conservation easement in the future. From 1990 to 1992, the Lyons family stopped negotiations with the Service because the Mapes Ranch was being considered as one of several potential locations for the site of a future University of California campus. After the Mapes Ranch was eliminated from consideration as a campus site, the landowners reentered acquisition negotiations with the Service; however, by that time, funding that would have allowed purchase of the entire Mapes Ranch in a single acquisition action had been redirected to other projects. Subsequent acquisition proceeded on a parcel-by-parcel basis as funds became available. Fee-title purchases were made of 861 acres in 1993, 662 acres in 1996, and 577 acres in 1997 using Migratory Bird Conservation Act funds. By 1997, the Service owned 2,877 acres within the Refuge.

In January 1997, a catastrophic flood occurred on the lower San Joaquin River system. Flood control levees failed and most of the Refuge and Faith Ranch, and much of the Mapes Ranch, were inundated by floodwaters. Other private lands west of the designated Refuge boundary also received extensive flooding. In all, the areas surrounding the Refuge suffered more than $2 billion in property damages. Subsequently, several landowners in the floodplain west of the San Joaquin River approached the Service with the intent of selling their flood-prone land for inclusion within the existing Refuge. This coincided with a Congressional mandate for the U.S. Army Corps of Engineers to explore nonstructural alternatives for flood protection; the same time period produced statewide initiatives, such as the San Joaquin River Management Plan, to restore riparian habitat and hydrologic function and provide alternate methods of flood control.

In support of these efforts, the Service proposed a nonstructural flood protection demonstration project in which it would acquire those flood-prone properties, breach or remove the existing flood control levee, and allow periodic floodwaters to spread over the Refuge-owned floodplain to reduce downstream flooding. This proposal grew into a multi agency effort, with the Service partnering with NRCS, U.S. Army Corps of Engineers, U.S. Bureau of Reclamation and the California Department of Water Resources. In 1997, the Service completed an environmental assessment and Land Protection Plan to expand the approved Refuge boundary to 12,887 acres. Following approval, in 1999 the Service acquired 2,037 acres of floodplain and riparian habitat west of the San Joaquin River in fee title, using a combination of Service (Emergency Flood Appropriations) and NRCS (Wetland Reserve Program) funds. In 2000, an additional 210 acres of floodplain habitat immediately south of and adjacent to the Refuge were acquired with CALFED funds, and 35 acres of riparian habitat along the Stanislaus River north of the Refuge were purchased by the Service Anadromous Fish Restoration Program and turned over to the Refuge for management. By 1998, the owners of the Mapes Ranch had reversed their original decision to sell their entire ranch in fee title, and instead, were willing to sell only a small portion of the remaining ranch lands in fee title and enroll the rest in perpetual conservation easements. Accordingly, the Service purchased Mapes Ranch lands both in fee title and in easement, and purchased a perpetual conservation easement on most of the Faith Ranch.

Fee Title Lands

Purchase of fee title land began in 1988 and is ongoing. The past five years have yielded the greatest increase in land acquisition for the Refuge. Figure 3 (Land Status Map) illustrates the approved Refuge boundary for acquisition, totaling close to 13,000 acres, and the current land ownership status. As of 2004, Fee title lands comprise 51 percent of the approved Refuge boundary. Sources of acquisition funds have included the Land and Water Conservation Fund, Migratory Bird Conservation Act Fund, CALFED Bay-Delta Program, emergency flood control appropriations, Anadromous Fish Restoration Program and the State of California.

Easement Lands

Easements are legal agreements whereby one party has binding authority regarding some aspect(s) of a property owner's land. Easements will influence the management activities and opportunities at the Refuge. In some cases, the Service has easements on adjacent private property; in other instances, other agencies have easements on Refuge lands.

Perpetual Conservation Easements (USFWS)

The Service acquired perpetual conservation easements on 1,834 acres of the 2,050 acre Faith Ranch in 2001, and 1,112.9 acres of the 4,000 acre Mapes Ranches in 2002. Additional funding is currently being sought to enroll much of the rest of the Mapes Ranch into the easement program. Both properties are within the Service's acquisition boundary for the Refuge. The purpose of the easements is to protect critical wintering habitat for Aleutian Canada geese, State threatened greater sandhill cranes, other threatened and endangered species, and migratory birds. The authority to acquire these easements comes from the 1997 Environmental Assessment for the expansion of the Refuge. These easements are subject to all Federal laws pertaining to those rights being acquired through the easement. Locally, the easements are administered by the San Luis NWR Complex under the guidance of the Easement Program Manager to ensure the ecological integrity of the easements are met.

The specific terms of the easements guide the landowners and the Service in protecting the integrity of the agricultural operations (irrigated and native pasture and cereal grains) while sustaining critical habitat for migratory wildlife. In addition, the Service acquired the right to continue providing wildlife habitat on the property if the landowner can no longer sustain a viable agricultural operation.

The Service is considering an acquisition boundary expansion concurrent with this CCP that would extend along the San Joaquin River floodplain from the southern boundary of the Refuge southward to the existing Grasslands Wildlife Management Area in Merced County. Under this proposal, most acquisitions would be perpetual conservation easements developed in conjunction with other agency easement programs. The Service has prepared a Study Report and drafted a Preliminary Project Proposal, and is seeking the authority to study land acquisition in this area. The Study Report is currently being reviewed within the Service.

Floodplain Warranty Easement Program (NRCS)

This NRCS easement applies to San Joaquin River NWR lands that the Service purchased from J. P. Lara and the El Solyo Ranch. This easement requires the Service and any subsequent landowner, to protect the floodplain and restore and manage for native habitats and natural resource values. The Lara and Vierra Units of the Refuge are both enrolled in this program and comprise 515.69 and 632.65 acres, respectively. The landowner (i.e., Refuge) is required to provide for "the unimpeded reach and flow of any waters in, over, or through the easement area; to retard runoff and prevent soil erosion through the restoration, protection, or enhancement of the floodplain; to restore, protect, manage, maintain, and enhance the functional values of wetlands, riparian areas, conservation buffer strips, and other lands; to conserve natural values including fish and wildlife habitat, water quality improvement, flood water retention, groundwater recharge, open space, aesthetic values, and environmental education; and to safeguard lives and property from floods, drought, and the products of erosion" in perpetuity.

To ensure the enrolled easement lands meet the program's purposes and goals, the management of these lands must conform to the Planned Conservation Treatment and Compatible Use Permit of NRCS. This permit between the NRCS and landowner addresses short-term management practices that would be applied until fulfilling the long-term goal of restoring riparian/wetland habitat and natural floodplain hydrology to maintain the ecological integrity of the easement are. The permit applies to both the Floodplain Warranty Easement and Wetlands Reserve Program Easements.

Wetland Reserve Easement Program (NRCS)

This NRCS-administered easement applies to lands west of the San Joaquin River that the Service purchased from Mr. Ed Hagemann *(Mehlhaff and Hay, 1999)*. It requires the owner to "restore, protect, manage, maintain, and enhance the functional values of wetlands and other lands, and for the conserving of natural values including fish and wildlife habitat, water quality improvement, flood water retention, groundwater recharge, open space, aesthetic values, and environmental education" for 30 years. The Hagemann tract of the Refuge is part of this program and comprises 2,017.8 acres. These lands are also required to conform to the Planned Conservation Treatment and Compatible Use Permit of NRCS, which is described above.

Refuge Management and Monitoring History

The level and type of management activities applied to the Refuge have evolved over time. Beginning in 1976, prior to Refuge establishment, graduate students or contract researchers were present on-site each winter during December to March to monitor the geese as part of the Aleutian Canada goose recovery program. The Service's Division of Research and Development (now the Biological Research Division of the U.S. Geological Survey) oversaw these monitoring efforts. The researchers collected goose population and distribution data and maintained a daily presence. They also monitored and reported any trespassing or poaching to landowners and Federal and State law enforcement

agents and conducted any necessary disease control activities.

This monitoring effort continued after the Refuge was established in 1987. The Aleutian Canada goose researchers provided daily on-site presence and relayed information regarding the geese and other Refuge issues to the San Luis NWR Complex headquarters in Los Banos. Following the acquisition of Christman Island in 1988, an entry gate was installed, access road improved and boundary signs posted. The management focus remained on Aleutian Canada geese even though the Refuge did not own lands suitable as goose habitat. The main issues at that time were the limited roost pond habitat on the Faith and Mapes Ranches due to prolonged drought and the presence of Aleutian Canada geese at the Modesto Sewage Treatment Facility, south of the Refuge, where they were exposed to recurring avian cholera outbreaks and experienced losses to that disease.

In 1991, the Service entered into cooperative agreements with the owners of the Faith and Mapes Ranches in which the Service compensated the landowners to flood wetlands on their properties to provide roost ponds for the geese. An additional agreement with the owners of the Faith Ranch provided that they would grow and mow down corn on their property as forage for Aleutian Canada geese. From 1991 to 1993, Service funds were not available and the landowners elected to provide those services at their own expense. During this same time, the Service contracted with U.S. Department of Agriculture–Wildlife Services to haze the geese at the sewage treatment facility to move them away from the disease outbreak sites. The combination of hazing and the provision of roost ponds and cereal grain forage were successful in getting the geese to shift back to the Refuge area.

With the acquisition of irrigated pasture, cropland and roost pond habitat in 1993, the Service gained a limited ability to manage for goose and sandhill crane wintering habitat on Refuge lands. To provide needed forage habitat, the Refuge entered into a cooperative agreement with the Lyons family. Under this agreement, the Cooperator planted and grew corn on a sharecrop basis and then harvested a share as silage. The Refuge's share of corn was grown to maturity, and then mowed down by the Cooperator on a schedule developed by the Refuge to provide forage for the geese. Cattle grazing was allowed on Refuge-owned irrigated pasture and uplands to create the short-grass foraging habitat preferred by Aleutian Canada geese and other arctic nesting geese, once they arrived in autumn/winter. The Cooperator compensated the Refuge for the value of grazing by planting winter wheat on Refuge lands to provide green forage for the geese (where the silage corn was harvested), and providing water to flood and maintain seasonal wetlands and roost ponds on the Refuge.

The amount of habitat available for goose and sandhill crane management increased as new lands were acquired from the Mapes Ranch. The existing Page Lake roost pond was enhanced through a cooperative project in 1996 by the Service, the Lyons family, and Ducks Unlimited, and additional roosting habitat (Goose Lake) was developed by the Service in 1999. By 1999, 335 acres of corn and winter wheat fields, 469 acres of irrigated pasture, 371 acres of native uplands, and 191 acres of roost ponds/wetlands were actively managed for Aleutian Canada geese, sandhill cranes, and other migratory birds on the Refuge. Although increasing numbers of geese made use of Refuge lands, there continued to be goose use at the Faith and Mapes Ranches.

In 1995, responsibility for monitoring wintering Aleutian Canada geese for the recovery program shifted to Region 1, Division of Refuges. Since that time, seasonal biologists of the San Luis NWR Complex have been based at the Refuge each winter to monitor Aleutian Canada geese and cackling Canada geese (*Branta canadensis minima*). While Refuge staff maintained the same level of goose monitoring as did the previous researchers, they were also available to perform other Refuge management activities. The staff increased disease control activities, took more control of water management, and initiated biological inventories, such as Refuge species lists, heron/egret rookery counts, sandhill crane counts, and vernal pool surveys.

Since 1996, a permanent Refuge staff member has been assigned the oversight and day-to-day management of the Refuge as a primary duty. This, and assistance from other San Luis NWR Complex staff, has allowed for an expansion of management activities at the Refuge. Management has included removing debris and unneeded facilities on new Refuge lands; demolishing buildings, including asbestos removal in Gardner's Cove and the former El Solyo Dairy site; repairing and upgrading lift pumps, pipelines, water control structures, and other water delivery facilities; developing new wetlands on former agricultural fields; initiating volunteer projects; constructing a cooperatively-funded observation tower for public use; preparing habitat restoration plans; and submitting major land acquisition and habitat restoration grant funding requests.

San Joaquin River on the Refuge.
Photo: USFWS

2 The Comprehensive Conservation Planning Process

The purpose of the Comprehensive Conservation Plan (CCP) for the San Joaquin River National Wildlife Refuge is to guide the management of the Refuge. The CCP provides managers with a 15-year strategy for achieving Refuge purposes and contributing toward the mission of the National Wildlife Refuge System, consistent with sound principles of fish and wildlife conservation and legal mandates. A CCP is required because the Refuge does not have a current plan that provides direction for managing wildlife, habitat and public uses.

This CCP for the Refuge is intended to meet the compliance requirements of the National Wildlife Refuge Improvement Act of 1997 (Improvement Act) and the National Environmental Policy Act (NEPA). Refuge planning policy also directed the process and development of the CPP, as outlined in Part 602, Chapters 1, 3 and 4 of the U.S. Fish and Wildlife Service Manual (May 2000).

The Refuge initiated the comprehensive conservation planning process in February 1999. Initially, members of the Complex staff and planning team identified preliminary issues, concerns and opportunities that were derived from wildlife and habitat monitoring and field experience associated with the past management of the Refuge. This preliminary list of issues, concerns and opportunities was further refined and developed through the planning process.

Service policy, the Improvement Act and NEPA provide specific guidance for the planning process, such as seeking public involvement in the preparation of the environmental assessment document.

This planning process included the development and analysis of "reasonable" management alternatives, including a "no action" alternative that reflects current conditions and management strategies. The CCP highlights the Service's preferred management alternative for the Refuge; other management alternatives were developed and considered as part of this planning process, and are found in Appendix B: Environmental Assessment.

The Planning Process

Part of comprehensive conservation planning includes preparation of a NEPA document. Key steps in the CCP and the parallel NEPA process are listed below:

1. Preplanning and team formation
2. Public scoping and involvement
3. Identifying issues, opportunities, and concerns
4. Defining and revising vision statement and Refuge goals
5. Developing and assessing alternatives
6. Identifying preferred alternative plan
7. Draft CCP and EA
8. Revising draft documents and releasing final CCP
9. Implementing the CCP
10. Monitoring/feedback

Figure 4 shows the overall CCP steps and process in a linear cycle, but the planning process is actually a non-sequential movement among the steps, with many revisions occurring during the development of the plan. The following sections provide additional detail on individual steps in the planning process.

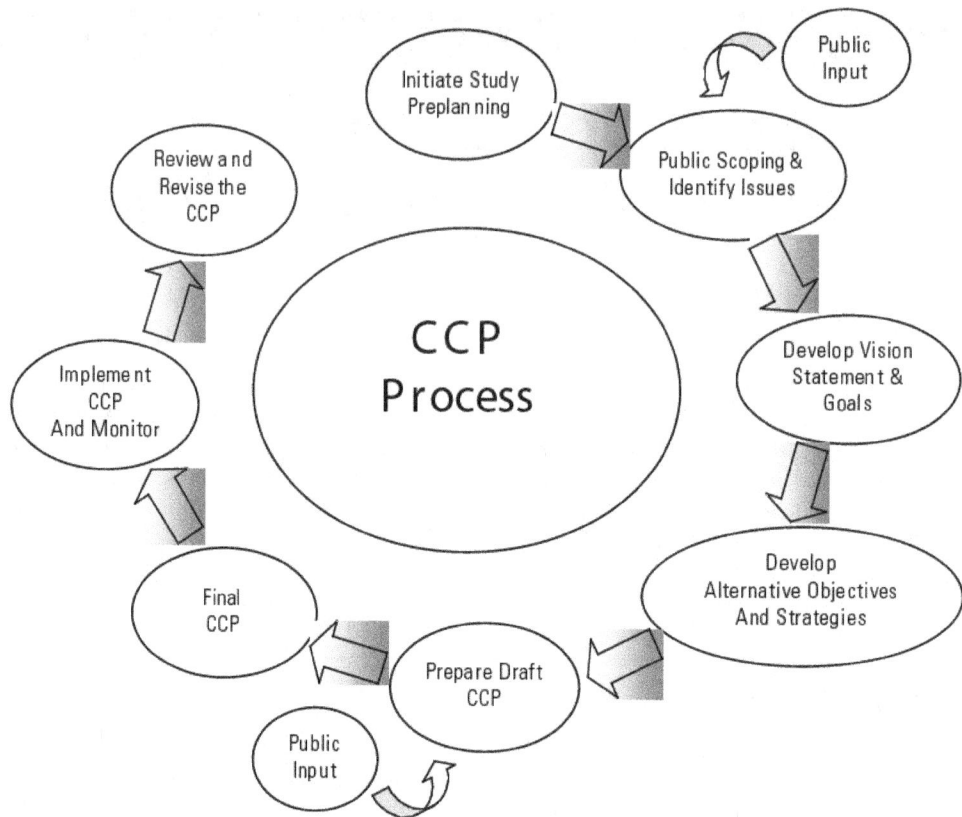

Figure 4: The Comprehensive Conservation Planning Process

The Planning Team

Two planning teams were created and used for this CCP. A core working team was formed to develop the majority of the documents and research background information. An expanded team was also formed comprising the core team, other Service staff, California Department of Fish and Game personnel and technical personnel to provide overview and guidance through the planning process. See Appendix M for the list of team members. As with all long-term projects, changes in the team membership occurred throughout the planning process.

Public Involvement in Planning

Public involvement is an important and necessary component of the CCP and NEPA process.

The Refuge held a public scoping workshop in March 1999 to further develop and ascertain planning issues for the Refuge.

The Refuge held quarterly Community Forum Meetings to keep the public and agencies informed regarding CCP progress and determine, refine and clarify Refuge issues. Several planning updates were mailed during this process to interested individuals, agencies, and organizations to apprise them of the planning progress and information generated. See Appendix C: Public Scoping and Involvement Process.

Overview of Public Scoping Comments and Discussions

The planning team identified issues, concerns and opportunities internally and through discussions with members of the technical panel, other key contacts and through the public scoping process. The team received comments in writing via regular mail and email.

The following key issues, concerns and opportunities were identified during the planning process and compiled by the

Service. Resource issues and opportunities were also identified during this process:

- Wildlife Management and Restoration
- Recreation and Public Use
- Refuge Staffing and Resources
- Flood Management
- Wetland and Water Management
- Refuge Proximity to Private Lands

The comprehensive goals, objectives and strategies of the CCP address all issues, concerns and opportunities raised by the public regarding management of the Refuge. See Appendix C: Public Scoping and Involvement Process and Chapter 5 for the proposed management alternative.

The draft CCP and EA have been provided to other agencies and the public for review and comment. Comments will be addressed and the document finalized for approval. Once the CCP has been approved, the Refuge can begin to implement the plan and associated step-down plans. Please refer to Chapters 5 and 6 of this document.

Development of Alternatives

The development of alternative management regimes for the San Joaquin River National Wildlife Refuge, assessment of their environmental effects, and identification of the preferred management alternative are described in Appendix B: Environmental Assessment (Figures 8–12). This CCP highlights the preferred management alternative for the Refuge.

3 Refuge Settings

Flyway Setting

The San Joaquin River NWR is situated within the Pacific Flyway. The flyway extends from the crest of the Rocky Mountains west to the Pacific Ocean within North America. It is used by millions of waterfowl and shorebirds for migration to and from wintering and breeding grounds. California's Central Valley is the largest watered flatland in the flyway, providing critical winter habitat for waterfowl, in particular. Autumn/winter rains and melting snow from the Sierra Nevada and Coast ranges provide water for wetlands, and mild winters make this area a major center for wintering waterfowl. Approximately 60 percent of the flyway's waterfowl winter in the Central Valley, with wintering duck populations ranging from two to five million birds. Common valley waterfowl species include the snow goose (*Anser caerulescens*), Ross' goose (*Anser rossii*), white-fronted goose (*Anser albifrons*), Aleutian Canada goose, green-winged teal (*Anas crecca*), northern shoveler (*Anas clypeata*), mallard (*Anas platyrhynchos*), northern pintail (*Anas acuta*), cinnamon teal (*Anas cyanopters*), gadwall (*Anas strepera*), American widgeon (*Anas americana*), canvasback (*Aythya valisinieria*), ring-necked duck (*Aythya collaris*), bufflehead (*Bucephala albeola*) and ruddy duck (*Oxyura jamaicensis*) (Root 1988).

The Central Valley is also a key region for many other waterbirds, including the sandhill crane (*Grus canadensis*), American coot (*Fulica americana*), moorhen (*Gallinula chloropus*), sora rail (*Porzana carolina*), Virginia rail (*Rallus limicola*), killdeer (*Charadrius vociferous*), black-necked stilt (*Himantopus mexicanus*), American avocet (*Recurvirostra americana*), greater yellowlegs (*Tringa melanoleuca*), spotted sandpiper (*Actitis macularia*), long-billed curlew (*Numenius americanus*), western sandpiper (*Calidris mauri*), least sandpiper (*Calidris minutilla*) and long and short-billed dowitchers (*Limnodromus scolopaceus* and *L. griseus*) (Root 1988, Shuford et al. 1998).

Ecoregion

The San Joaquin River NWR is situated in the Central Valley/San Francisco Bay Ecoregion. The Central Valley is an elongate depression that lies between the Coast Ranges and the Sierra Nevada Mountains. It is approximately 400 miles long and 40 miles wide. Historically, three principal habitats dominated this ecoregion—valley grasslands, wetlands and riparian woodlands/forests. Valley grasslands consisted of perennial grasses and dominated the landscape, comprising 81 percent of the area (Schoenherr 1992). Wetlands were associated with rivers and streams and widespread in low elevation areas, comprising approximately 15 percent of the ecoregion (Schoenherr 1992). Wetlands, particularly seasonal wetlands, were fed by winter rains and runoff from the surrounding mountain ranges. Riparian woodlands and forests, frequently associated with rivers and streams, encompassed four percent of the ecoregion (Schoenherr 1992). Wildlife of the ecoregion was diverse, with grassland-dependent species, including large grazers, which were a dominant component of the community. The ecoregion's large wetland element provided significant habitat for large concentrations of waterfowl, shorebirds and other waterbirds.

Following settlement and in the past 150 years major changes have occurred

Refuge lands were historically a mosaic of riverine channels, broad riparian floodplains, wetlands and grassland savannas dominated by valley oaks.

in the ecoregion. Today, the ecoregion has been converted into one of the most productive agricultural areas in the world *(Schoenherr 1992)*. With this increase in land devoted to agricultural use there was an associated loss of wildlands. The valley grasslands dominated by native perennial grasses that once covered all well-drained areas now only occur in a pristine condition on just one percent of the ecoregion *(Schoenherr 1992)*. Likewise, approximately 94 percent of the wetlands and 89 percent of the riparian woodlands/forests have also disappeared *(Schoenherr 1992)*. Despite these losses, the remaining wildlands in the ecoregion still provide significant habitats for unique Central Valley wildlife communities; they also offer critical habitat for many wildlife species both regionally and nationally, particularly waterfowl and other waterbirds.

Historic Refuge Environment

Refuge lands were historically a mosaic of riverine channels, broad riparian floodplains, wetlands and grassland savannas dominated by valley oaks. This area was bisected by the main stem of the San Joaquin River and was bounded to the north by the Stanislaus River and to the south by the Tuolumne River. Historically, the San Joaquin River and its tributaries would overtop natural levees and inundate the floodplain following winter rains and Sierra snow melt. This system was dynamic, depositing rich alluvium, creating and cutting streambanks, creating and maintaining riparian forests, creating oxbow lakes and backwater sloughs by changing the rivers' course, clearing and depositing debris, scouring streambeds, and exposing and depositing gravel and sand. The resulting floodplain corridor was vegetated by trees, such as button willow, black willow and sandbar willow in the lower areas. The upper areas were dominated by box-elder, Fremont's cottonwood, Oregon ash, arroyo willow and valley oak. The most common mid- and ground-story shrubs included California rose, California blackberry, elderberry and wild grape. Dominant grasses and forbs included creeping

wild rye, basket sedge, mugwort and goldenrod. The uplands adjacent to the floodplain were less frequently inundated by floods and were dotted with valley oaks with an understory of perennial grasses and forbs, such as creeping wild rye, saltgrass, alkali sacaton, gum plant and spikeweed. Wetlands and vernal pools were abundant throughout the upland savannahs. These habitats supported a wide array of migratory birds, salmonids and other fish, large herbivores and other wetland and upland associated wildlife.

American Indians lived in permanent villages on elevated locations above the floodplain. These native people, the Yokuts, made their homes along the San Joaquin River and its tributaries in part, because of the abundance of natural resources in the area. When Lieutenant Gabriel Moraga led the Spanish cavalry into the San Joaquin Valley in 1805, the explorers were astonished by the abundance of wildlife. The Spaniards saw ducks, geese, cranes, herons, pelicans, curlews, pronghorn antelope, tule elk and grizzly bears, in large numbers.

Conditions began to rapidly change by the 1850s, following European settlement and development. Pronghorn antelope were extirpated, tule elk were nearly made extinct and other wildlife were diminished by commercial hunting that was driven by the meat markets of San Francisco and mining camps of the California Gold Rush. Valley oaks and riparian forests were cut down for lumber and firewood to fuel steamboat traffic on the rivers. By the late 1800s and early 1900s, wetlands were being drained, creeks channelized and floodplains cleared of trees to create farmland.

During the 1940s and 1950s, Friant Dam and other water storage/flood control facilities were built on the San Joaquin River and its major tributaries, and water diversions were made for agricultural, industrial and metropolitan uses. Flood control levees were constructed along the river's course to contain and greatly narrow the floodplain. Nearly two centuries after Moraga's expedition, the San Joaquin Valley landscape is dominated by agriculture and is now one of the most intensively farmed regions in North America.

The Refuge area was drastically altered, but to a lesser extent than most of the lands along the San Joaquin River. Levees were built on both sides of the river. To the west, White Lake was drained, Ingram and Hospital Creeks channelized and much of the floodplain cleared for orchard and row crop agricultural development in the early 1900s; however, the riparian forest and associated sloughs on Christman Island and along both sides of the river corridor were retained. East of the river, much of the floodplain and adjacent uplands was cleared of trees and converted to grazing lands for cattle. Stock ponds were developed and natural slough channels were maintained to provide water for cattle. Eventually, much of the eastern land was leveled, canals and pipelines were constructed for irrigation, and native grass/forb plant communities were replaced by domestic pasture grasses.

Habitat alteration has continued into recent times. Valley oaks and other trees in the river corridor were cut down in the 1960s and 1970s, one-third of the riparian forests on Christman Island were cleared in the 1980s, and much of the pasture land was converted to row crop agriculture in the 1980s and 1990s. Even with these recent developments, the area provides critically important habitat for a wide array of wildlife species. The river channels and associated oxbows serve as migration corridors and rearing habitat for salmonids and other fish species. The riparian forest and fallow fields provide migration and nesting habitat for neotropical birds and other riparian associated species. The uplands provide foraging and roosting habitat for migratory birds, such as waterfowl, cranes and shorebirds.

Special Status Lands and Wilderness
The Refuge is located on the northern boundary of the Grasslands area, which contains the largest remaining acreage of freshwater wetlands in California. The importance of this critical area for waterfowl and other waterbirds has been recognized by the Central Valley Joint Venture and the North American Waterfowl Management Plan. It is considered of international importance for migratory waterfowl and shorebirds of the Pacific Flyway. This area also provides key habitats for several priority species listed in the Service's list of Birds of Conservation Concern *(USFWS in preparation)*. Because of its value to wildlife, the San Joaquin River NWR functions as a northern extension of the Grasslands area.

The San Joaquin River NWR is not considered a federal wilderness study area as it does not meet wilderness designation criteria (Appendix N). The Refuge contains no special status lands.

Climate
The San Joaquin Valley lies between the Coastal Range and the Sierra Nevada Range. Well-protected from the Pacific Ocean, the area displays continental climate characteristics of hot, dry summers, with mild winters. Its location on the western edge of the continent protects the region from the weather extremes found farther inland. The climate of the valley promotes widespread grasslands. Precipitation occurs during winter and spring months, but is reduced because of the rain shadow effect of the Coast Range. Patterson, a town near the Refuge, has an average annual rainfall of approximately 10 inches. The San Joaquin Valley has a frost-free growing season of 270 to 300 days. The average temperature ranges from a low of 38 degrees F to a high of just over 100 degrees F; however, extreme temperatures, as low as 20 degrees and as high 115 degrees, have been recorded. Cold-air drainage from the surrounding mountains becomes trapped, forming a persistent inversion layer in the valley. During winter this is manifested in a dense, ground-hugging fog known as tule fog. Summer days are hot and hazy. Air quality of the Central Valley is poor.

Soils and Geology

Schoenherr (1992) provides a broad overview of the soils and geology of California's Central Valley:

"The Central Valley is a huge basin filled with sediments. The deepest parts of the gravels and sands are marine sediments that have accumulated since the late Jurassic—145 million years ago. The sea retreated from the Central Valley at about the same time that the southern Coast Ranges were uplifted, and during the long history of accumulation of marine sediments in the valley, the basement rock continued to subside. During most of the Pleistocene the area was occupied by shallow brackish and freshwater lakes. During the last 5 million years, sediments accumulated as alluvial deposits washed out of the mountains. These deposits are only a few thousand feet deep over most of the valley floor."

Physical conditions at the Refuge, especially the geology of the watersheds, are different on lands east or west of the San Joaquin River. A soil survey for eastern and western Stanislaus County used the San Joaquin River to delineate a boundary (*McLauglin and Huntington 1968*). Refuge lands on both sides of the river consist primarily of recent alluvial floodplains and basin lands. Soil types are often mixed alluvium mapped as soil associations. Basin soils are affected by high water tables from river water seepage, as well as saturation of the land by deep penetration of rain and irrigation water. Most soils exhibit very poor drainage, with a high water table at a depth of just three to six feet from December through April *(Arkley 1964)*. If the land is irrigated, it provides prime farmland, although it floods every few years.

Topography and River Geomorphology

Elevations on the Refuge vary from 20 feet along the edge of the San Joaquin River to 40 feet in several locations near the eastern boundary. The Refuge is bisected by the San Joaquin River, which has flood control levees on both banks. Most of the Refuge lands along the river have been laser-leveled and intensively farmed in the past for row crops and irrigated pasture. Small parcels that retain the natural topography are present on the East Unit (for Refuge management purposes the area east of the San Joaquin River is referred to as the East Unit and lands west of the river as the West Unit). The riparian corridors inside the levees were not intensively developed and retain their natural topography. Within the levees, the sizes of the riparian areas range from narrow corridors to large floodplains of 900 acres or more (i.e., Christman Island and Gardner's Cove areas). A remnant of what used to be the main river channel is present on the West Unit and forms the western boundary of Christman Island.

Two major tributaries of the San Joaquin River occur on the East Unit. The Stanislaus River is located along part of the Refuge's north boundary where it flows into the San Joaquin River. The Tuolumne River forms the southern boundary of the East Unit and flows into the San Joaquin River near the Refuge's southern end. Both rivers contribute significant flows to the San Joaquin River system and both have been modified by levees, gravel mining and water diversions, but to a lesser extent than the San Joaquin River.

Eight smaller tributaries cross western Stanislaus County, draining from the eastern slopes of the Diablo Range to the San Joaquin River. From north to south they are: Hospital, Ingram, Kern, Del Puerto, Salado, Crow, Orestimba and Garzas creeks. These creeks have watersheds of similar size and are spaced three to five miles apart. Though rainfall is infrequent in these creek watersheds, it is often heavy, making them prone to erosion. None of the creeks flow continuously. Two of these, Hospital and Ingram creeks, cross the West Unit of the Refuge. Both have been heavily channelized on farmland located upslope from the Refuge and essentially, act as agricultural drains. Agricultural tailwater makes up the largest contribution of flows entering the Refuge from the watersheds of these two creeks.

Nearly all Refuge lands have been separated from river flood water by human-made levees. The course of the San Joaquin River has been modified and channelized to enhance water delivery and flood control. Modification, levee construction and water diversions to enhance water deliveries and flood control throughout the San Joaquin River system have greatly altered the hydrology and fluvial processes, such as river meandering *(Katibah 1984)*. Except for extreme flood events that result in levee failure, water in the river remains within the levee corridor and does not spread across the floodplain. These fluvial processes are reduced most years, even in the riparian areas inside the levee corridor, because the river flows are reduced from historic levels.

Drainage

Due to the low elevation of Refuge lands and the location of natural river channels, numerous sources of surface water drain onto the Refuge. Field drains, community ditches and tributaries of the San Joaquin River collect surface and subsurface drainage from nearby agricultural fields. Several irrigation districts that supply irrigation water to upslope farmlands also operate and maintain drainage channels that flow into the Refuge as water proceeds to the river.

In the East Unit, several lateral canals from Modesto Irrigation District terminate on or adjacent to the Refuge and contribute intermittent flows to the Refuge or the San Joaquin River. The Riley Slough portion of the East Unit is saturated year round due to the high water table and tail-water from adjacent pasture lands.

On the West Unit, drainage rights and maintenance costs have been recorded in legal documents by previous landowners for several locations on the Refuge. White Lake Mutual Water Company pays 35 percent of drainage facility maintenance and pumping costs for the drainage ditch system over Refuge lands purchased from Ed Hagermann. White Lake Mutual Water Company has drainage rights over

those lands arising from a 1941 drainage easement in the deed conveying the land from Burkhard Investment Company to the predecessor of Hagermann (i.e., Pietro Rampone).

West Stanislaus Irrigation District obtained a memorandum of agreement on May 8, 1928 with Burkhard Investment Company. The agreement was amended in 1939. The agreements address the right of access and construction for the West Stanislaus Irrigation District intake channel, as well as the obligation to protect the Refuge land from canal seepage. West Stanislaus Irrigation District also has an obligation to operate drainage pumps on Refuge property purchased from J. P. Lara. The 1928 agreement refers to "maintain the water level and seepage from the main canal at 22 U.S.E.D. and at least eight feet below the natural, average ground level, the district to install, maintain the necessary pumps and operate the pumping of the seepage water." Access across the West Stanislaus Irrigation District canal is required by installation and maintenance of three pile bridges by the District. The West Stanislaus Irrigation District has expressed a desire to revise the 1928 drainage agreement to eliminate the pumping and bridge maintenance requirements.

On February 12, 1947 West Stanislaus Irrigation District obtained an agreement for "use of a strip of land for ditch and road purposes" 30 feet wide. This agreement provides "free ingress, egress and regress" for West Stanislaus Irrigation District along a route generally parallel to Hospital Creek. The agreement allows West Stanislaus Irrigation District to construct "a ditch of twenty (20) cubic feet per second capacity..." and provides for West Stanislaus Irrigation District to maintain the ditch, culvert pipes and road right-of-way on Refuge lands.

The agricultural drainage water carries suspended sediment that tends to drop out of the water as flows slow down on the flat basin land near the San Joaquin River. Over time the deposition of sediment causes water to back up in the creek channel.

Maintenance of drainage channels is a concern to the West Stanislaus Irrigation District, adjacent private landowners, Turlock Mosquito Abatement District, as well as the Refuge (Figure 6–Wetland Units Map).

Flood Management

Most of the Refuge lands are within the 100-year floodplain of the San Joaquin River. Historic records indicate the area is subject to periodically significant rainfall and flooding. Damaging floods occurred in 1937-38, 1950-51, 1952, 1955-56, 1962-63, 1982-83, 1986, 1995, 1996-97 and 1998. Expanding the Refuge west of the San Joaquin River was motivated by a desire to expand the floodplain and associated riparian habitat beyond the existing levees.

All Refuge lands in the West Unit are within the 100-year floodplain of the San Joaquin River and subject to inundation during floods. This entire unit (at the time private land) was inundated due to levee failure during the January 1997 flood. Some lands in the West Unit were within Reclamation Districts 2099, 2100 and 2102 prior to their acquisition by the Service. When the Service acquired lands in the West Unit, those Reclamation Districts were disbanded. Lands in the East Unit are within Reclamation District 2031, which experienced extensive flooding during 1997. The environmental assessment (EA) of the effects of expanding the San Joaquin River NWR was completed in 1997. Part of the EA identified Refuge participation in a partnership with the Natural Resource Conservation Service (NRCS), U.S. Army Corps of Engineers (Corps), California Department of Water Resources and California Reclamation Board regarding a nonstructural flood control project for the Refuge. This project involved acquiring lands protected by Corps levees and breeching the levees in up to seven locations to allow future floods to inundate the new Refuge lands which, in turn, would provide flood protection to areas downstream by offering temporary storage of peak flood flows. The temporary flooding of the Refuge lands would also return a more natural flood regime to the San Joaquin River floodplain and support the riparian habitat that benefits from periodic inundation. Another component of implementing the nonstructural flood control alternative is the Corps' acquisition of flowage easements from landowners adjacent to the three reclamation districts (Appendix H: Levee Breach Study). A Corps project report selected this nonstructural flood control project as the best flood control proposal for the area in response to damage caused by the January 1997 flood.

Water Quality

Water quality in the San Joaquin River is degraded by irrigation drainwater and urban runoff during summer and by flushing of accumulated pollutants in urban stormwater and other runoff in the winter. The California State Water Resources Control Board (SWRCB) designated 100 miles of the San Joaquin River, including the reach in Stanislaus County, as an impaired water body in 1990 (SWRCB 1990). In addition, the lower San Joaquin River, from Mendota Pool to Vernalis (130 mile stretch of the River including the Refuge), is currently listed as impaired in accordance with Section 303(d) of the Clean Water Act, for exceeding salinity and boron water quality objectives. Portions of the watershed upstream of the Refuge are listed under the Clean Water Act for organophosphorus pesticides, diazinon, chlorpyrifos and selenium (Regional Water Quality Board 2002). The greatest problems occur on the River and its tributaries upstream of its confluence with the Merced River. At the Refuge and downstream, relatively cleaner waters from Merced, Tuolumne and Stanislaus rivers flow into the San Joaquin River, which improves overall water quality. Nevertheless, water quality levels for some contaminants in the San Joaquin River upstream of the Refuge are still some of the highest in the nation (USGS 1998).

The Refuge is located in a reach of the San Joaquin River that has also been identified as the main contributor of nonpoint source sediment in the San Joaquin River. Erosion from agricultural irrigation is the main contributor of the sediment, producing 1.2 million tons of sediment per year. Organochlorine pesticides, such as DDT, are adsorbed in the sediment carried by the tailwater and transported to the San Joaquin River.

Although there is substantial data on water quality for the four rivers that flow into the Refuge, little data has been collected from the Refuge's smaller waterways, including the lateral canals that enter the Refuge from agricultural and urban lands. Contaminants monitoring data is not yet available for the sloughs and managed wetlands. In July 1999 the Service's Contaminants Branch of the Sacramento Fish and Wildlife Office conducted a one-time survey on the lands west of the San Joaquin River. The report concluded that further monitoring was warranted, organochlorines should continue to be a concern to the Refuge and the Vierra Dairy should be closed (*USFWS 1999*).

Vegetation

The Central Valley contains three major plant communities—riparian, wetland and grassland—all of which occur at the San Joaquin NWR *(Schonenherr 1992)* (Figure 5–Land Cover Map). Within each habitat group, the Refuge identified communities using Smith et al. (1995), Sawyer and Keeler-Wolf (1995) and DFG (1999); they include great valley oak riparian, black willow riparian forest, permanent wetland, semipermanent wetland, seasonal wetland, vernal pool, tilled cropland, irrigated pasture and native grassland (Figure 5–Land Cover Map and Table 1–Existing Habitat Cover Types).

Riparian Habitats
Great Valley Oak Riparian
Oak woodland once covered much of the landscape surrounding the San Joaquin River NWR; however, only a remnant of this habitat remains. Most of the oak woodland was destroyed by logging, ranching or conversion to agricultural fields. Most of California's oak woodlands were relatively stable during the long period of use by American Indians. Beginning with European settlement approximately 150

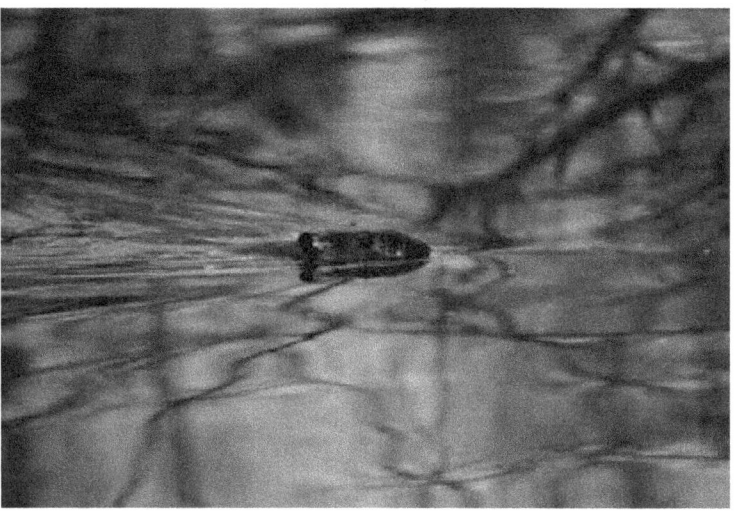

Beaver crossing waterway; good water quality is a critical issue for many wildlife at the Refuge.
Photo: Jerry Baldwin

years ago, oak densities and their dominance declined in California due to the introduction of livestock and land clearing for intensive agriculture *(McShea and Healy 2002)*.

Virtually all of the great valley oak riparian community on the Refuge occurs within the flood control levees. The overstory is dominated by mature valley oaks, with varying amounts of Fremont cottonwood (*Populus fremontii*), box-elder (*Acer negundo*) and willow (*Salix* spp.) present. The understory is dominated by creeping wild rye (*Leymus triticoides*), basket sedge (*Carex barbarae*), California rose (*Rosa californica*), California blackberry (*Rubus ursinus*), and in more open areas, mugwort (*Artemisia douglasiana*) and western goldenrod (*Euthamia occidentalis*). Although individual and scattered groves of valley oaks are present on the floodplain and adjacent uplands, most were previously cleared for agricultural development.

The largest valley oaks and best examples of this community type are present at the Gardner's Cove area, Christman Island, Colwell Bottoms and the former Lara property. Grazing and public use have suppressed the regeneration of oaks and other riparian species in the Gardner's Cove area; yet, during the past decade, the cessation of those land uses and the presence of soil scarification (i.e., clearing and soil turning) due to flooding (1997 and 1998) have

Figure 5: Land Cover Map

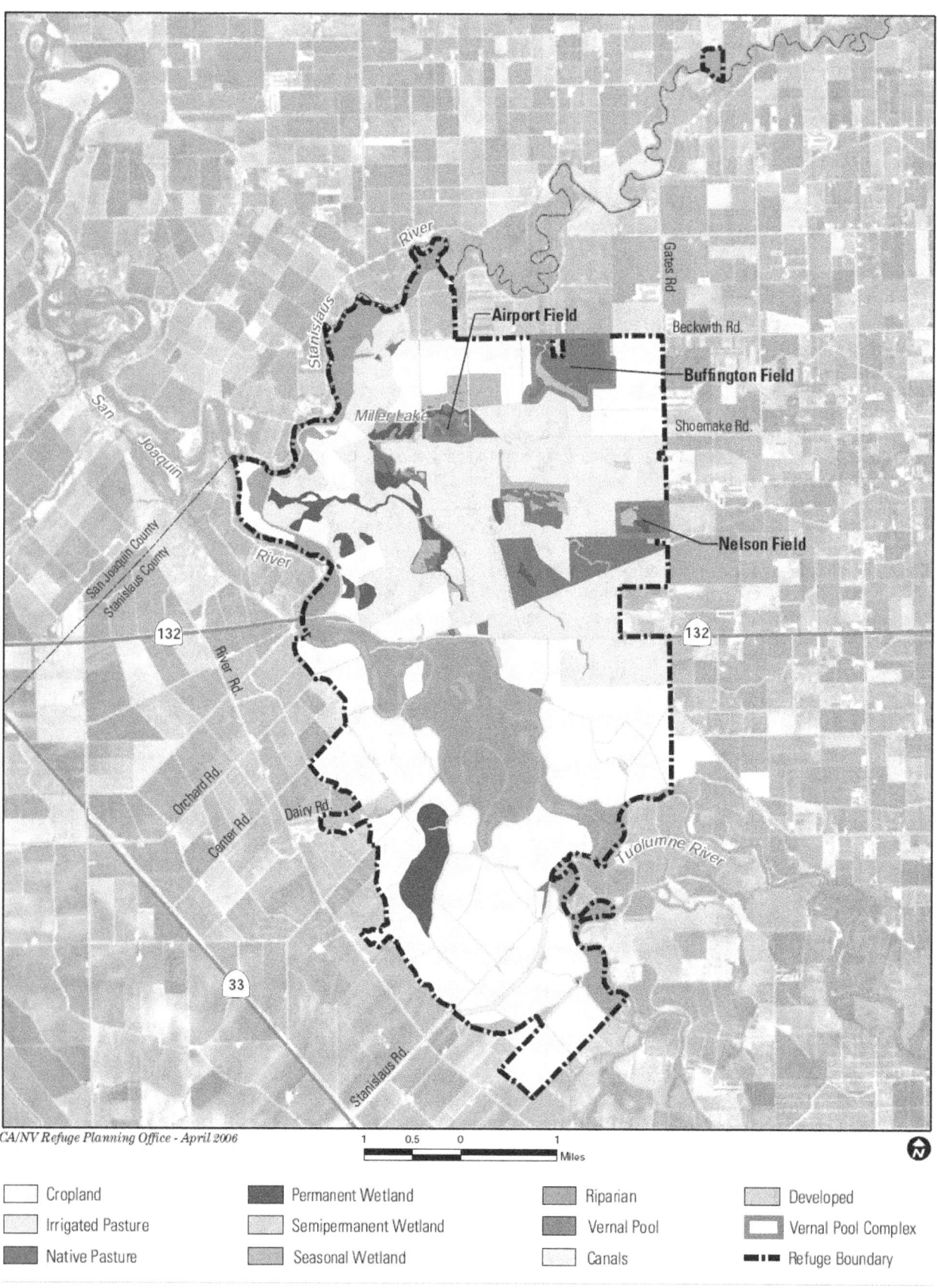

CA/NV Refuge Planning Office - April 2006

Cropland

Irrigated Pasture

Native Pasture

Permanent Wetland

Semipermanent Wetland

Seasonal Wetland

Riparian

Vernal Pool

Canals

Developed

Vernal Pool Complex

Refuge Boundary

allowed previously suppressed valley oak seedlings/saplings to begin to grow. Valley oak and other hardwood trees are naturally regenerating, and a native understory of mugwort, goldenrod, basket sedge, creeping wild rye grass, wild rose and California blackberry have become more common and, in most places, have excluded nonnative vegetation *(Griggs 2000)*. Great valley oak saplings are naturally regenerating on Christman Island and a few other locations on the Refuge; however, in other locations, perennial pepperweed (*Lepidium latifolium*), an invasive nonnative weed species, has become established and is expanding rapidly in the oak woodland understory.

Black Willow Riparian Forest
The woody overstory of this vegetative community, which typically grows along water courses, is dominated by black willow (*Salix gooddingii*) with varying amounts of sandbar willow (*Salix hindsiana*), box-elder, buttonbush (*Cephalanthus occidentalis*) and Oregon ash (*Fraxinus latifolia*) *(Ornduff 1974)*. Widely-spaced individual or small groups of Fremont cottonwood (*Populus fremontii*) are present and black walnut (*Juglans hindii*) occurs in a few locations.

The black willow riparian forest community at the San Joaquin River NWR occupies much of the river corridor inside the levees along the San Joaquin, Tuolumne, and Stanislaus rivers, as well as Hospital and Ingram creeks which drain into the San Joaquin River. The quality of riparian habitat that currently exists on the Refuge is highly variable due to stand age and successional stage. Black willow riparian forest on the Refuge is classified into early and late successional habitats. Early successional habitat often occurs in retired farmland that was inundated by the floods of 1997 and 1998. Young black willows and cottonwoods dominate these areas. Scattered coyote bush has become established as well. Forbs include mugwort, goldenrod, and nettle (*Urtica dioica* var. *holosericea*); however, invasive weeds, such as poison hemlock (*Conium maculatum*), perennial pepperweed, and

Table 1: Existing Habitat Cover Types

Habitat Cover Type	Acreage
Cropland	744
Permanent Wetland	342
Riparian	1,919
Wet Meadow	0
Seasonal Wetland	218
Irrigated Pasture	506
Native Grassland	372
Semi-Permanent Wetland	132
Vernal Pool	4
Developed	56
Fallow	2,098
Irrigation / Drainage Canal	197
Total:	**6,588**

Johnson grass (*Sorghum halepense*), now dominate the understory of some areas. The late successional habitat is characterized by a greater diversity of trees and a more developed understory consisting of California blackberry, California rose, basket sedge and forbs. Introduced invasive weeds are present in varying degrees in much of these riparian areas.

Wetlands
Permanent Wetlands
Permanent wetlands are those that remain flooded all year and support hydrophytes (water-loving plants)—either herbaceous or woody species *(Gritsch and Gosselink 2000)*. These wetlands at the San Joaquin River NWR are ringed by a perimeter of emergent vegetation, such as hardstem bulrush (*Scirpus acutus*) and/or cattail (*Typha latifolia*); oxbows are bordered by riparian forest. Permanent wetlands cover approximately 340 acres of the San Joaquin River NWR. Wetlands that have been present for decades include Miller Lake, Quesma Field and Nelson Lake, which are situated on the northern unit of the Refuge. Oxbow lakes occur near Gardner's Cove and Christman Island. In 1999, changed drain pump management in a former agricultural field allowed the naturally high water table and irrigation

run-off from neighboring agricultural lands to inundate the site and form White Lake. A permanent wetland, which fluctuates with the level of the San Joaquin River, also exists on the west side of the Refuge.

Semipermanent Wetlands
Semipermanent wetlands are flooded most of the year but are dry during late summer to early winter *(Smith et al. 1995).* There are 132 acres of semipermanent wetlands on the Refuge, including the upper benches of Riley Slough, part of an abandoned field on the southwest corner of the Refuge and oxbow sloughs along the San Joaquin River. Bulrush and cattails thickly vegetate these areas; the oxbows are ringed by riparian forest.

Seasonal Wetlands
Seasonal wetlands are flooded during autumn and maintained throughout the winter until drawdown occurs in spring *(Smith et al. 1995).* A total of 218 acres of managed seasonal wetlands currently occur on the Refuge. Depending on the water regime, the dominant vegetation is swamp timothy (*Heleochloa schoenoides*), watergrass (*Echinochloa crusgalli*), smartweed (*Polygonum* spp.), sprangletop (*Leptochloa fascicularis*) and cockleburr (*Xanthium strumarium*). Seasonal wetlands on the East unit of the Refuge include Page Lake, Watergrass Unit and Goose Lake, which are maintained for roosting and feeding ponds for Aleutian Canada geese and other migratory birds. In addition, seasonal wetlands develop on former agricultural fields in the West Unit of the Refuge on an irregular basis due to high flows in the San Joaquin River, rainfall and upslope drainage of irrigation water.

Shorebirds are dependent on wetlands such as this black necked stilt.
Photo: Jerry Baldwin

Vernal Pools
Vernal pools are a unique wetland that can be found in the shallow basins of valley grasslands where an impermeable soil layer causes a perched water table to form *(Ferren and Pritchett 1988).* They become filled by winter rains and dry in the spring by evaporation. Showy wild flowers, such as downingia (*Downingia* spp.) and goldfields (*Lasthenia* spp.), bloom as the pools dry, but during the summer, the basins are bare except for prostrate plants, such as annual atriplexes (*Atriplex* spp.). The plants and animals of vernal pools, including the federally-listed endangered vernal pool fairy shrimp (*Branchinecta lynchi*) and vernal pool tadpole shrimp (*Lepidurus packardi*), are highly restricted to specific locations and are dependent on this shallow basin habitat for their survival *(Jain and Moyle 1981).*

Based on examination of 1938 aerial photography, vernal pools were once common on lands within the Refuge acquisition boundary east of the San Joaquin River. Today only a remnant survives on the few parcels of land where the topography has not been altered. Four acres of vernal pools in three locations occur on Refuge lands (Figure 4–Land Cover Map). A vernal pool complex of 14 pools, ranging in size from 51 to 562 square yards, is present on the Buffington Field unit. Some vernal pools were eliminated or altered prior to Service ownership. On the south and west sides of the vernal pool complex, small channels were installed to connect and deliver water to several shallow pools, which are now filled with vegetation typical of a seasonal wetland. A raised dirt road in the center of the field divides one vernal pool into halves.

A smaller complex of three vernal pools is present in the Airport Field next to Miller Lake. Invertebrates associated with vernal pools have been found in one of the pools. Pools are also present in the uplands adjacent to Nelson Lake; although these are characteristic of vernal pools, no vernal pool invertebrates have been found in surveys.

Grasslands (Uplands)

Native Grasslands

Native grasslands on the Refuge consist of lands with native undulating topography modified by small channels and berms, but not land-leveled. Central Valley grassland habitats have been severely altered over the past one hundred and fifty years. Exotic annual grass species, principally of Mediterranean origin, replaced the native perennial grasses that likely once dominated these grasslands. Many annual exotics, including ripgut brome, soft chess, wild oats and others, now prevail on the grasslands; however, native grassland species, such as alkali sacaton, saltgrass and spikeweed, are still common in some areas. Restoration of native habitats, including these grasslands, is a critical element for Refuge management. Noxious weedy species, such as yellow starthistle and pepperweed, are also beginning to invade some of these habitats. Aggressive control of exotic species is critical to maintain native habitat.

Tilled Cropland

Tilled croplands consist of lands that have been converted from a more natural condition by land-leveling and installation of pipelines for irrigation, and are under active management for agricultural crop production. The Service acquired close to 3,000 acres of tilled croplands. The majority is presently in fallow condition and will be restored to a combination of native upland, riparian and wetland habitats. A small portion of tilled cropland remains on the Refuge to produce winter forage for Aleutian Canada geese, sandhill cranes, and other migratory birds. Most of the Refuge tilled croplands are east of the San Joaquin River and planted to corn (grain forage) and winter wheat (green browse forage). Privately owned tilled croplands within the Refuge acquisition boundary are planted to these and other cereal grains, alfalfa, tomatoes, beans, and melons for commercial production.

Fallow Field

Fallow fields are tilled croplands that have been taken out of active agricultural production. No irrigation water is applied to these sites and the land develops a cover of weedy, mostly nonnative, broadleaf plants. The Service has purchased close to 3,000 acres of formerly tilled cropland that has been allowed to lie fallow. Most of the Refuge-owned fallow fields are on the west side of the San Joaquin River. Fallow fields will be restored as funds permit to a variety of natural habitats, including riparian forest, wetlands and grasslands. Very little fallow field habitat is present on private lands within the acquisition boundary of the Refuge east of the San Joaquin River.

Irrigated Pasture

Irrigated pasture consists of lands that have been converted from a more natural condition by land-leveling, installing pipelines to facilitate flood irrigation, and planting a mixture of domestic grasses and legumes. They are maintained by frequent irrigation and are typically grazed by cattle year round, following a rotational cycle that averages about eight months of grazing per year. The Service has purchased approximately 500 acres of irrigated pasture as part of the Refuge; irrigation has been continued to provide shortgrass foraging habitat for Aleutian Canada geese, sandhill cranes and other migratory birds.

Wildlife

California's diverse terrain and vegetative communities provide conditions for a high degree of wildlife diversity. San Joaquin Valley NWR contains elements of the Central Valley's three major vegetative types and has the potential to provide habitat for over 325 species of wildlife. Appendix E provides a species list of fish and wildlife on the Refuge. A significant portion of the Refuge consists of fallow agricultural lands; their planned restoration has the potential to increase the number of wildlife species and their abundance over the present distribution and abundance on the Refuge.

Invertebrates

The Refuge provides habitat for both aquatic and terrestrial invertebrate species. Past invertebrate surveys have been limited to the sampling of vernal pools for the presence of tadpole and fairy shrimp, but it is believed that the aquatic and terrestrial invertebrate fauna is representative for the Central Valley. Non-systematic field observations have detected the presence of representatives from nine of the thirteen insect orders with aquatic species *(Merritt and Cummins 1996)*, as well as two types of native bees. Future work on invertebrates is dependent on funding and may include surveys for the endangered valley elderberry longhorn beetle (*Desmocerus californicus dimorphus*) and native bee inventories.

Fish

Habitats for fish on the Refuge include rivers, permanent wetlands, oxbows and sloughs. Three major rivers (i.e., San Joaquin, Tuolumne and Stanislaus) join on the Refuge and provide an important nexus for migratory fish. The stretch of the San Joaquin River and tributaries on the Refuge provide habitat and connectivity to aquatic habitats for a wide range of fish, including fall-run chinook salmon (*Oncorhynchus tshawytscha*), steelhead (*Oncorhynchus mykiss*) and Sacramento splittail (*Pogonichthys macrolepidotus*)—all species which are or proposed for federal listing under the Endangered Species Act. Appendix E provides the species list of fish known to occur or have the potential to occur at the Refuge.

Historically, California supported over 90 freshwater species of native fishes; the Sacramento-San Joaquin Valley sustained approximately 60 native species *(Schoenherr 1992)*. Although there is still a diversity of aquatic habitats in the Central Valley, the natural assemblages of Central Valley fish communities have been degraded by altered flow regimes, levee construction/maintenance and associated loss of floodplain, reduction in riparian habitats, the introduction of exotic fish species and other factors. At San Joaquin River NWR, many native fish species have been extirpated or are severely reduced in number, but several still occur, including fall-run chinook salmon,

steelhead, Pacific lamprey (*Lamptera tridentata*), river lamprey (*Lamptera ayresi*), hitch (*Lavinia exilicauda*), Sacramento splittail, Sacramento blackfish (*Orthodon microlepidotus*), Sacramento sucker (*Catostomus occidentalis*), tule perch (*Hysterocarpus traski*), and prickly sculpin (*Cottus asper*). Some of these species are dependent on large river systems while others use sloughs and other backwater habitats. Introduced species now dominate many of the aquatic habitats of the Central Valley, including those at San Joaquin River NWR. Thirty-six introduced fish species are present in the Central Valley *(Schoenherr 1992)*. Refuge aquatic habitats are now dominated by the following non-native species: black bass (*Micropterus salmoides*), carp (*Cyprinus carpio*), bluegill (*Lepomis macrochirus*), threadfin shad (*Dorosoma petenese*), red shiner (*Cyprinella lutrensis*) and striped bass (*Morone saxatilis*).

Although the Refuge was originally established to benefit endangered and other migratory birds, it has the potential to benefit and enhance populations of native fish. The restoration of floodplain habitats on the Refuge, including riparian forest, and a return to more natural water regimes have the potential to benefit many natives dependent on floodplains for spawning and rearing purposes *(Moyle 2002)*.

Amphibians and Reptiles

San Joaquin River NWR has the potential for twenty-seven species of reptiles and amphibians to occur (Appendix E). Semi-arid regions such as the Central Valley frequently possess diverse communities of both lizards and snakes; by contrast, whereas the turtle and amphibian communities generally have a low species diversity *(Schoenherr 1992)*. The most easily observable Refuge species include the western pond turtle (*Clemmys marmorota*), western fence lizard (*Sceloporus occidentalis*), racer (*Coluber constrictor*), Pacific gopher snake (*Pituophis melanoleuscus*), common garter snake

(*Thamnophis sirtalis*) and introduced bullfrog (*Rana catesbeiana*).

A preliminary survey of reptiles and amphibians was conducted at the San Joaquin River NWR in 1998; the survey was not meant to be all encompassing, but to focus on reptile/amphibian use of major habitats. The survey indicated low overall capture rates, but documented 13 of the 27 species of reptiles and amphibians with the potential to occur on the Refuge. The survey detected reptile and amphibians in woodlands and native grasslands, but none in fallow agricultural fields.

Birds

The San Joaquin River NWR was initially established due to its importance to migratory birds, particularly the Aleutian Canada goose. The Refuge has the potential to provide habitat for all the avian species known to occur in the Central Valley, which includes over 225 species of birds.

The most spectacular bird use at the Refuge is by waterbirds, especially waterfowl. Close to 30 species of ducks, geese and swans make use of the Refuge and the most common include the Aleutian Canada goose, snow goose, white-fronted goose, green-winged teal, northern shoveler, mallard, northern pintail, cinnamon teal, gadwall, widgeon and ruddy duck. Other conspicuous Refuge waterbirds include the pied-billed grebe (*Podilymbus podiceps*), double-crested cormorant (*Phalarcrocorax auritus*), white-faced ibis (*Plegadis chihi*), white pelican (*Pelecans erythrorhyncos*), sandhill crane, American coot, moorhen, killdeer, black-necked stilt, American avocet, greater yellowlegs, western sandpiper, least sandpiper, as well as long and short-billed dowitchers. Colonial nesting waterbirds maintain colonies on the Refuge, such as the great blue heron (*Ardea herodias*), great egret (*Ardea alba*) and double-crested cormorant.

Aside from waterbirds, the Refuge is an important area to many other resident and migratory bird species. Many species of neotropical migrants have been detected on the Refuge, including the lazuli bunting (*Passerina amoena*), blue grosbeak (*Guiraca caerulea*), ash-throated flycatcher (*Myiarchus cinerascens*), western wood-pewee (*Contopus sordidulus*), black-headed grosbeak (*Pheucticus melanocephalus*), Savannah sparrow (*Passerculus sandwichensis*), horned lark (*Eremophila alpestris*), yellow warbler (*Dendroica petechia*), Nashville warbler (*Vermifora ruficappilla*), orange-crowned warbler (*Vermivora celata*), yellow-rumped warbler (*Dendroica coronata*), Pacific-slope flycatcher (*Empidonax difficilis*), and ruby-crowned kinglet (*Regulus calendula*) (Appendix E). A survey was conducted for the yellow-billed cuckoo (*Coccyzus americanus*), a rare species in the Central Valley, but none was found, although the Refuge does fall within its historic range *(Sawyer, et al. 1997, Gains and Laymon 1984, Laymon 1998)*. Compared to other habitats, oak woodlands and riparian habitats, which support multiple

Drake northern shoveler.
Photo: Jerry Baldwin

vegetation layers, have the highest diversity of bird species on the Refuge. Typically, natural habitats supported the greatest diversity of bird species, whereas crop fields and fallow agricultural lands supported few birds *(Hammond et al. 2002).*

Mammals

California hosts an array of mammals principally due to the state's large size and variety of habitats. Over 200 species of mammals have been documented in California, one of the largest state species counts in the nation *(Zeiner et al. 1990).* Before European settlement, tule elk (*Cervus elaphus nannoides*), grizzly bear (*Ursus arctos*), pronghorn antelope (*Antilocapra americana*), California black-tailed deer (*Odocoileus hemionus*), mountain lion (*Felis concolor*) and bobcat (*Felis catus*) were conspicuous in the Central Valley. The mammal composition today is quite different, however, due to the loss of suitable habitat, over-harvest and introduction of nonnative plants and animals. Most of the aforementioned large mammals are no longer found in the area.

Rodent and rabbit species make up the largest segment, approximately one third, of the mammals found on San Joaquin River NWR as in most areas *(Eisenberg 1982).* Three rabbit species occur on the Complex, including the desert cottontail (*Sylvilagus audubonii*),

Coyote, a conspicuous predator at the Refuge.
Photo: Gary Powell

black-tailed hare (*Lepus californicus*) and endangered riparian brush rabbit (*Sylvilagus bachmanii riparius*). Both the hare and the desert cottontail are conspicuous species at the Refuge. Large rodents, which are also conspicuous on the Refuge, include the aquatic muskrat (*Ondatra zibethicus*) and beaver (*Castor canadensis*) – both of which leave obvious signs and play important roles in aquatic systems. Dominant rodents at the Refuge, which also act as keystone species because of their grazing/seed predation and/or tunneling, include the deer mouse (*Peromyscus maniculatus*), California vole (*Microtus californicus*) and California ground squirrel (*Spermophilus beecheyi*). The endangered San Joaquin Valley woodrat (*Neotoma fuscipes riparia*), as well as the introduced black rat (*Rattus rattus*), also occur on the Refuge

An inventory of the bat community has not been conducted at the San Joaquin River NWR, although by potential species number they make up a sizable component of the mammalian fauna. The most common species probably include the big brown bat (*Eptesicus fuscus*), western pipistrelle (*Pipistrellus hespornus*), little brown bat (*Myotis lucifugus*) and Brazilian free-tailed bat (*Tadarida brasiliensis*).

Although the largest carnivore species of the Central Valley were eliminated during the settlement period, mid-size and small carnivores are prevalent at the Refuge and comprise approximately one fifth of the potential mammalian community. The most common carnivores/omnivores on the Refuge include the coyote (*Canis latrans*), raccoon (*Procyon lotor*), striped skunk (*Mephitis mephitis*), northern river otter (*Lutra canadensis*), longtailed weasel (*Mustela frenata*) and Virginia opossum (*Didelphis virginiana*) while the gray fox (*Urocyon cinereoargenteus*) and mink (*Mustela vison*) are present, but rarely encountered.

Other mammals that occur on the Refuge include the ornate shrew (*Sorex ornatus*)

and mule deer (*Odocoileus hemionus*), and several domestic mammals which either trespass onto the Refuge or are used in the Refuge's grazing program. A permanent mule deer population does not exist at the San Joaquin River NWR, although transient deer are periodically observed.

Threatened and Endangered Species

Several threatened and endangered species occur or have the potential to occur on the San Joaquin River NWR. The Refuge was originally established for the Aleutian Canada goose, which was listed as endangered in 1967. Much of the population had been ravaged by arctic foxes introduced onto the Aleutian Islands in Alaska where this subspecies breeds *(USFWS 1991)*. The population numbered 800 birds when the Aleutian Canada Goose Recovery Program was implemented in the 1970s. Since then, breeding islands have been cleared of foxes, captive-breeding programs started and implemented and geese reestablished on fox-free islands. By 1991, the Aleutian Canada goose population had recovered to more than 7,000 birds and, as a subspecies, was down-listed to threatened status. By 1998 the population numbered more than 28,000 and the process of delisting Aleutian Canada geese from threatened status began. More than 95 percent of the world's Aleutian Canada goose population winters on the Refuge. Most years, Page Lake is the main roost pond. Aleutian Canada geese also use Nelson Lake and the new Goose Lake. Annual monitoring of these birds has been conducted as part of the Aleutian Canada Goose Recovery Program since 1976. Corn and winter wheat are planted on the Refuge annually to provide forage for the increasing population. Aleutian Canada geese populations have recovered dramatically and have been delisted as a federally threatened species. Managing and monitoring the Aleutian Canada geese population continues on the Refuge. Existing roost ponds have been improved and expanded to potentially reduce deaths from avian cholera by physically spreading out the population. These improvements and others would further minimize avian cholera mortality and local crop depredation, and discourage poaching.

The federally listed endangered species that occur or which could potentially occur on the Refuge include the riparian brush rabbit (*Sylvilagus bachmani riparius*), San Joaquin Valley woodrat (*Neotoma fuscipes riparia*), San Joaquin kit fox (*Vulpes macrotis mutica*), bald eagle (*Haliaeetus leucocephalus*), least Bell's vireo (*Vireo bellii pusillus*), giant garter snake (*Thamnophis couchi gigas*), chinook salmon, Sacramento splittail, steelhead trout, valley elderberry longhorn beetle (*Desmocerus californicus dimorphus*), vernal pool fairy shrimp, and vernal pool tadpole shrimp.

The riparian brush rabbit is a subspecies of the brush rabbit. Its original distribution was the most limited of all the brush rabbit subspecies, restricted to a small stretch of the San Joaquin River and some of its tributaries (*Orr 1940*). Presently, the riparian brush rabbit only occurs in three isolated populations, none of which is considered secure for maintaining the long-term status of the population. Plans call for reestablishing a population on the San Joaquin River NWR through a captive breeding program *(Williams et al. 2002)*. Existing riparian vegetation at the Refuge, coupled with planned restoration of riparian habitat on the Refuge, will provide this subspecies the largest block of contiguous habitat in its existing range.

The San Joaquin Valley woodrat uses similar habitat as the riparian brush rabbit. Unlike the rabbit, the woodrat has not disappeared from the Refuge and small numbers of the woodrat occur. The planned riparian habitat restoration will benefit not only the rabbit but the endangered woodrat, as well.

No records exist for the San Joaquin kit fox on the Refuge, although there are records within 20 miles. Bald eagles are routine Refuge visitors, particularly during the winter months, and are usually attracted to the large concentrations of waterfowl. Least Bell's vireo nested in recently planted riparian habitat at the Refuge in 2005. Planned riparian restoration activities will likely produce additional suitable habitat for this endangered songbird. The giant garter snake is listed as endangered and requires permanent water as habitat. Although suitable habitat appears to exist on the Refuge, there have been no documented records for the species. All three species of listed or candidate fish species – Chinook salmon, steelhead and Sacramento splittail—occur on the Refuge. The valley elderberry longhorn beetle is dependent on elderberry (*Sambucus mexicanus*) for its life cycle. Little elderberry habitat exists on the Refuge but the small amount that does occur may support populations of the endangered beetle. Two vernal pool listed shrimp have been documented at some of the Refuge's vernal pools; these habitats will be maintained in perpetuity on the Refuge.

State of California listed endangered and threatened species which occur on the Refuge include the greater sandhill crane, yellow-billed cuckoo, Swainson's hawk, willow flycatcher and bank swallow. The greater sandhill crane annually winters on and around the Refuge. Existing pastures, agricultural lands, and wetlands are used for foraging and roosting *(Lewis 1979, Reinecke and Drapu 1979, Iverson et al. 1982, Walker and Schemnitz 1987)*. Unlike lesser sandhill cranes, greater sandhill cranes within the Pacific Flyway have shown precipitous population declines because of destruction of wetlands and riparian habitat, lack of nesting habitat, and low productivity *(Pogson and Lindstedt 1991)*. This area is one of eight geographic regions in which greater sandhill cranes winter in the Central Valley. The yellow-billed cuckoo, which relies upon riparian woodland, and the willow flycatcher, which depends on wet, shrubby habitat, have not recently been documented on the Refuge, although planned habitat restoration activities will likely create additional habitat for these species. The bank swallow require large cut banks for its breeding colonies; although such areas exist at the Refuge, there have been no bank swallow colonies during the last decade. The Swainson's hawk is conspicuous at the Refuge, which provides habitat for several breeding pairs.

Historical and Cultural Resources

Cultural resources are physical remains, sites, objects, records, oral testimony and traditions that connect us to our nation's history and the land's past. Cultural resources include archaeological and historical artifacts, sites, landscapes, plants, animals, sacred locations and cultural properties that play an important role in the traditional and continuing life of a community.

Little formal cultural resources survey work has been conducted on the Refuge. The known cultural resources in and within one mile of the acquisition boundary of the San Joaquin River NWR consist of eight prehistoric sites and two historic sites. Cultural resources, especially archaeological sites, are fragile and nonrenewable. Most consist of worked stone, fire-altered rocks and organically enriched soil on or close to the surface. When compared to the surrounding landscape and contemporary cultural features, such as roads, ditches and structures, archaeological sites are small and subtle.

Prehistory

The Refuge is in the homeland of several Indian groups collectively known as the Northern Valley Yokuts. Within the Refuge, one group, the Tuolumnes aboriginal group, has been identified. The Tuolumnes' home was east of the San Joaquin River, between the Stanislaus and Tuolumne rivers *(True 1981)*. The Refuge borders the territory of, and at various times, was probably occupied by, the Miwok tribe *(Silverstein 1978)*. As neighbors, the Yokuts and Miwok traded, intermarried and shared many cultural practices. Acorns (valley oak) and salmon were dietary staples, as were tule elk, antelope and jackrabbit *(Levy 1995)*. Major Northern Valley Yokuts settlements were located within a short distance of the San Joaquin River banks and along major tributaries. As the San Joaquin and Tuolumne rivers have changed and meandered considerably over the years, these sites may appear most anywhere on the Refuge. Villages were typically built on ground higher than the surrounding area, situated to best exploit the rich subsistence resources without being consistently flooded. Yokuts would mainly congregate in the winter; during spring, summer and fall, groups would disperse to gather different resources *(Jensen 1996)*. Villages were typically a scatter of four or five to several dozen structures. Each house served as a home to one family. Large villages might also have a great communal earth lodge for ceremonial use.

History

Spanish colonization of California began with the readily accessible coastal areas, avoiding the interior valleys during the 18th century. Early in the 19th century, military explorers and missionaries moved away from the coast and to the inland valleys. Early settlement by the Spanish in California was accomplished through the mission system, where livestock and farming were mainstays. The arrival of the Spanish into California shifted the use of the land from hunting/gathering to an agrarian use. By the 1820s many Native Americans were assimilated into the mission system. The Spanish also introduced both cattle and sheep into California; at the height of the mission period, there were 400,000 cattle and 300,000 sheep *(Schoenherr 1992)*. During the late 1840s, there was a decline in the Spanish/Mexican influence in California, particularly during the gold rush years; however, livestock production continued as a major agricultural activity. Due to a rapid increase in miners and settlers during the gold rush years, numbers of livestock were vastly increased to meet this new demand; by the 1860s, there were 3 million cattle and 9 million sheep in the state. Damage to California's rangeland from overgrazing was extensive by the 1870s and it has never fully recovered *(Schoenherr 1992)*. Agriculture continued to be the primary land use of the Central Valley into the 1900s. Dry farming (i.e., farming without irrigation) for wheat became popular in the late 1880s but declining wheat prices brought an end to this practice during the 1920s. Irrigated agriculture in the Central Valley was common in the 1850s but became widespread during the 1900s, as it is today. The Central

Valley remains an agricultural center as it was under the Spanish. The primary agriculture products from the Central Valley are dairy products, beef, grapes, rice, orchard crops and cotton. Hay and alfalfa production for livestock are also common agricultural products.

Refuge Facilities

Most existing facilities at the San Joaquin River NWR were on the land prior to acquisition by the Service to establish and develop the Refuge. Conditions of the facilities vary greatly and range from very good to hazardous. Some facilities and structures are being used and maintained, while others need to be removed.

Roads

There are numerous public roads within and surrounding the approved Refuge boundary (Figure 6–Refuge Roads & Facilities Map). The Refuge is partially bounded by Beckwith Road to the north, Gates Road to the east, and Dairy and Pelican Roads to the southwest. The Refuge is bisected by Highway 132. Shoemake and Page Roads (nonpublic) traverse the approved Refuge boundary.

In addition to public roads, the Refuge contains many interior roads, many of which are unpaved. Most of these roads are shared with other parties, such as the Faith and Mapes ranches. Two paved roads that run through the Refuge are the West Stanislaus Road and an unnamed road that extends south off Shoemake Road. There are no existing walking trails on the Refuge.

Buildings

There are twenty-four buildings/structures on the Refuge. These structures are concentrated on the west side of the Refuge, particularly the Vierra, Hagerman and Lara Units. These structures range from milk barns to pole sheds, livestock run-in shelters, houses, and railroad cars. All of these were acquired with the land when purchased for the Refuge. Most of the buildings and structures are in poor condition and were not maintained for many years. The three exceptions are houses

Figure 6: Refuge Roads and Facilities

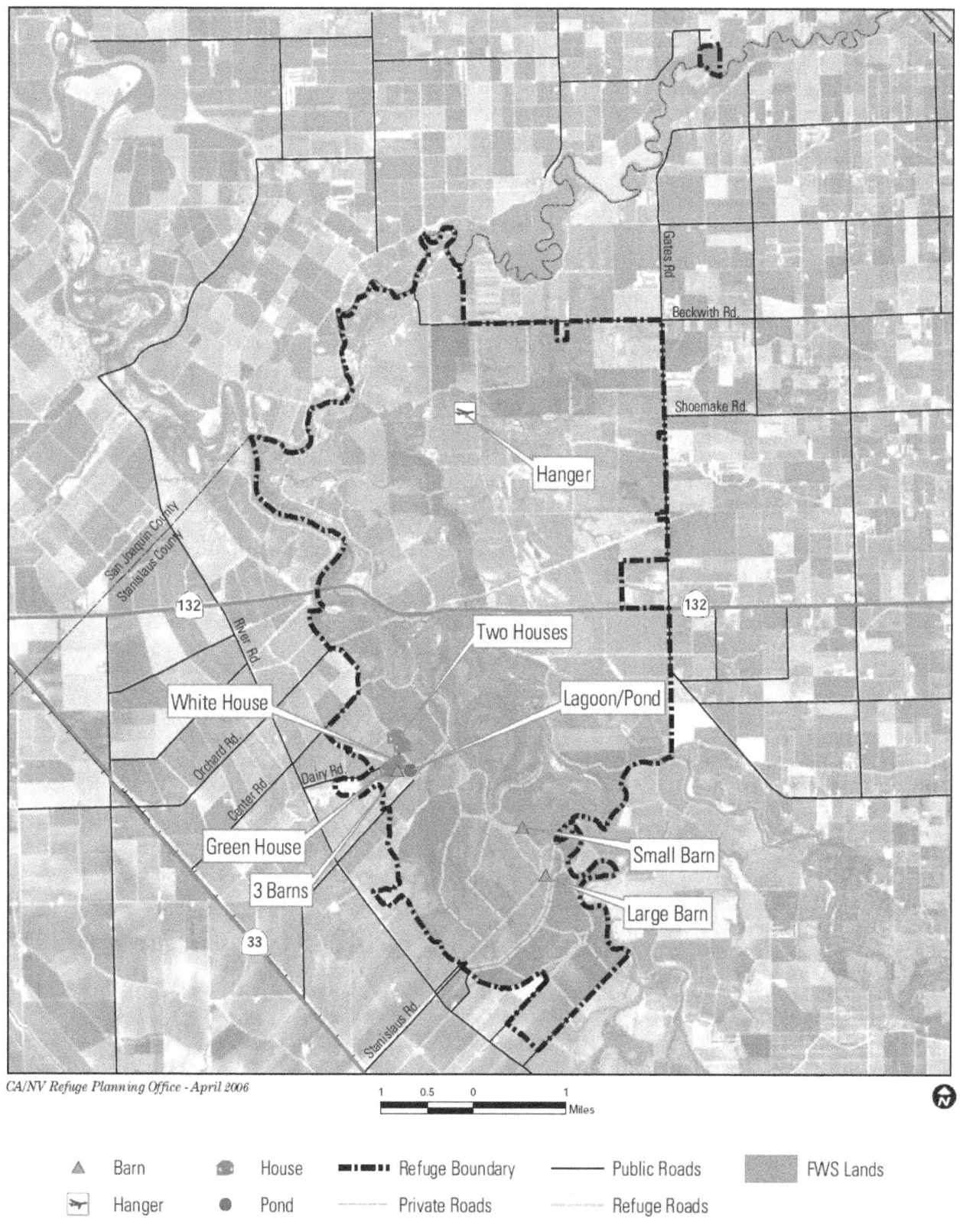

in good condition, one of which is a life estate, one a government quarters and the remaining used as the office for the Refuge. The majority of the buildings and structures are a safety hazard and an attractive nuisance and need to be removed.

Wetland Units and Water Infrastructure

Most of the facilities now owned by the Refuge are old and are in varying conditions of usability. Many lift pumps and pipelines on both the East and West units were damaged during the January 1997 flood. In addition, the reliability, cost and quality of water provided by these facilities has a wide range of variability (Figure 7–Wetland Units). To date, much of the operational water delivery for Refuge wetlands and uplands management has been driven by the configuration and condition of the agricultural wells, pumps, pipelines and canals that were in place at the time of purchase. In part of the East Unit, water is provided by lift pumps and wells, or conveyed by pipelines and canals, owned by the Mapes Ranch as part of their CLMA with the Refuge. Refuge-owned water production facilities in the East Unit include: a lift pump next to the MID Main Drain and another along Riley Slough (both rehabilitated after the 1997 flood); a 70 h.p. agricultural well at the Dairy Field (installed by the Refuge in 2000); a domestic well at the Quesma Field wetlands (condition uncertain); and a lift pump along the Tuolumne River (damaged in 1997 flood and needs to be rehabilitated and fitted with a fish screen before operation). Water is conveyed to Refuge wetlands and uplands via a network of pipelines, concrete lined ditches and earthen canals. Portions of the MID Main Drain, MID Lateral 4, and MID Lateral 7 water delivery canals run through or adjacent to Refuge lands. Most of the managed wetland units have inlet and outlet structures that have been installed since 1993 and all have staff gauges to facilitate water management.

A total of 12 lift pumps, six drain pumps, nine domestic wells, and one agricultural well were present on West Unit lands when acquired by the Service. Many of these facilities are currently inoperable due to damage from the 1997 flood. Three lift pumps (two 50 h.p. and one 34 h.p.) along the West Stanislaus Irrigation District Intake Canal were rehabilitated and fitted with fish screens in the summer of 2001 to use for habitat restoration and management. The Refuge plans to rehabilitate and screen additional lift pumps to meet restoration and management needs, but others will be abandoned. The drain pump at the White Lake outlet was rehabilitated in 2000 and is used to manage water levels of White Lake wetlands and to meet Refuge drainage obligations to the White Lake Mutual Water Company. Five domestic wells were filled and capped in 2001. The remaining wells are operational and are being used for restoration purposes, but water quality concerns associated with these wells, as well as test wells drilled in 2001, will limit the use of ground water for long term management of Refuge lands. An agricultural well on the southern end of the unit (former Arambell and Rose property) is currently being used to irrigate alfalfa grown on the Refuge through a CLMA. The water quality of that well is unknown. The West Unit is overlaid by a network of pipelines and canals that were used to deliver and drain off irrigation water to the former agricultural fields. Part of these facilities will be maintained and used for habitat restoration and subsequent management. Canals and pipelines that are not needed for management purposes will be filled in or blocked (pipelines) as part of the habitat restoration efforts.

Visitor Facilities

A wildlife viewing platform, information kiosk and associated parking lot located off of Beckwith Road are available to the public for wildlife observations. These facilities were constructed in 2002 and provide the only public use facilities at the Refuge

Current Management Activities

Most of the past habitat management, wildlife management, and biological monitoring and research at the Refuge were focused on supporting the recovery goals for Aleutian Canada geese. As the Refuge's

Figure 7: Wetland Units

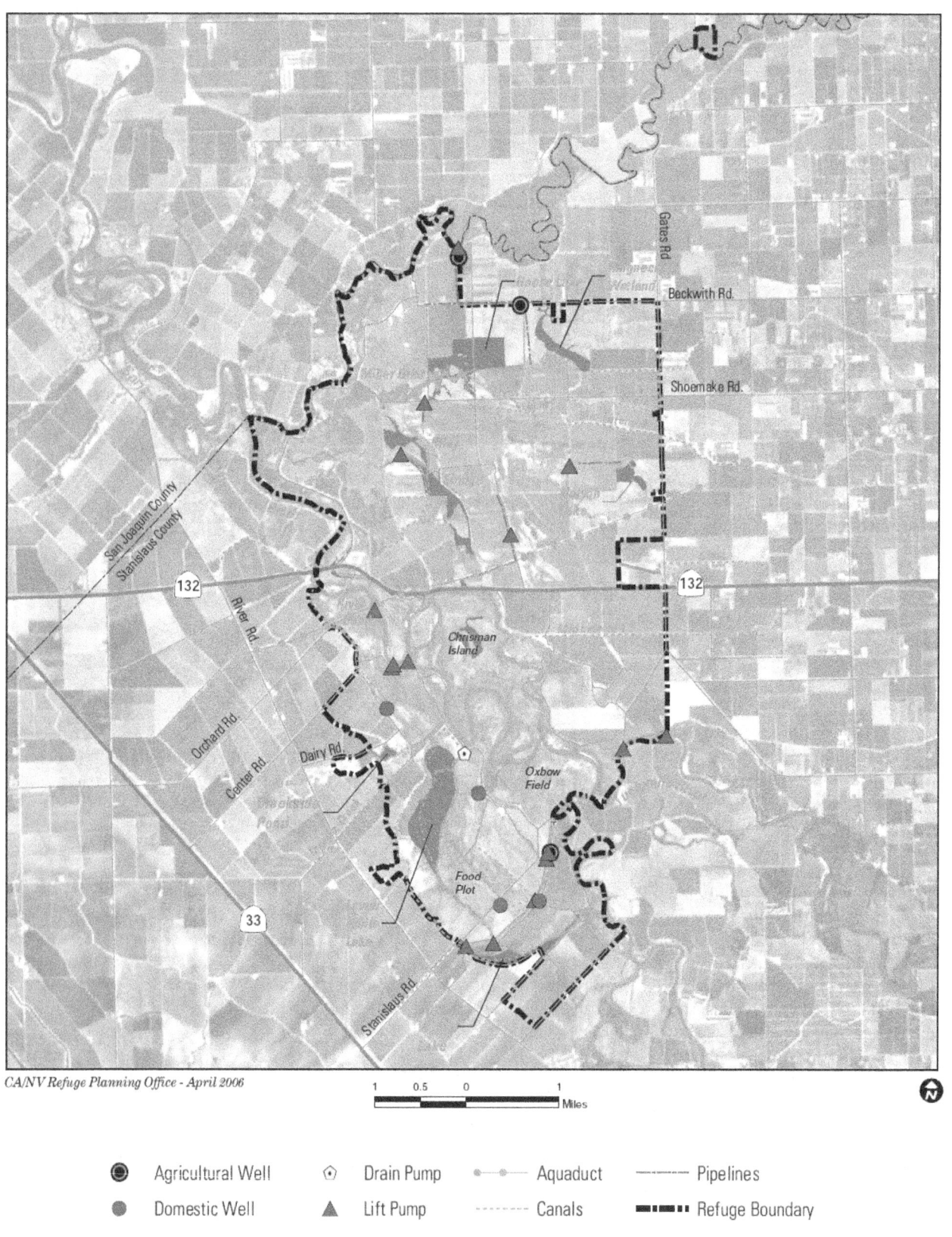

1   0.5   0   1
Miles

⬤ Agricultural Well	⊙ Drain Pump	•—•— Aquaduct	——— Pipelines
⬤ Domestic Well	▲ Lift Pump	------ Canals	■■■•••■■ Refuge Boundary

land base increased and additional staff support became available, these activities were expanded to include additional species and other resource concerns. Management changed after acquisition of the large floodplain area west of the San Joaquin River. Currently, the Refuge is actively managing upland and wetland habitats, as well as restoring the riparian floodplain, for the benefit of endangered species and migratory birds. Refuge management units are identified on Figure 8.

Habitat Management
Wetland Management

Water management is required for most of the wetlands on the San Joaquin River NWR due to alteration of the original or natural hydrology of the area for agricultural and urban purposes and needs. Water for managed Refuge wetlands is supplied through various lift pumps on the San Joaquin, Stanislaus and Tuolumne rivers, deep wells, Modesto Irrigation District supplies, operational spill, and tailwater from adjacent farming operations. It is conveyed via irrigation district, privately-owned, or Refuge-owned canals and other infrastructure (Figure 6. Wetland Units). Most of the wetland units have staff gauges in place to monitor water levels. Current water management practices have developed over time based on land acquisitions, partnerships, location in the Modesto Irrigation District service area, legal drainage obligations to upslope landowners, pumping constraints due to anadromous fish and the availability of operating funds to pay power costs. Refuge wetlands are managed as single units or complexes, as described below (Figure 7. Wetland Units Map).

Page Lake Complex

The Page Lake complex consists of Page Lake, Goose Lake, Watergrass Unit and Upper Miller Lake. Water is supplied from the Stanislaus River via a lift pump owned and operated by the Lyons family, a deep well owned by the Refuge, and operational spill from the end of the Modesto Irrigation District system. The management objective of Page and Goose lakes is to serve as winter roost habitat for Aleutian Canada

geese and other migratory birds. Both lakes are drawn down in mid-April and not irrigated during the summer. The pond bottoms become vegetated with swamp timothy. In autumn, the lakes' islands, shorelines and any tall vegetation, such as cocklebur, are mowed prior to floodup to provide loafing habitat and to maintain the open character necessary for goose roost ponds. Page and Goose lakes are flooded in early October prior to the arrival of Aleutian Canada geese and water levels are maintained through the winter. The Watergrass Unit, immediately west of and an extension of Page Lake, is managed to provide foraging habitat for ducks in the winter and shorebirds in spring. Irrigation tailwater from Refuge cornfields (grown as goose forage) immediately north of the unit is allowed to drain into the unit to promote a thick stand of watergrass. It is flooded in October with the arrival of waterfowl, and then drawn down slowly in April (as are Page and Goose lakes) to provide mudflat foraging habitat for migrating shorebirds. Miller Lake, immediately south of Page Lake and the Watergrass Unit, is managed as a permanent wetland. It is ringed by cattail and roundstem bulrush and provides habitat for grebes, marsh nesting birds and other wetland dependent wildlife.

Nelson Lake Complex

East and West Nelson lakes are managed as a complex of seasonal and permanent wetlands. These units are situated within the Modesto Irrigation District service area. Water is supplied by the irrigation district from spring through fall, and by a well owned and operated by the Lyons family during the winter. East Nelson Lake is the deepest (three to six feet deep) and is the only permanent pond in the unit. West Nelson Lake is a seasonal extension of East Nelson Lake and averages approximately 12 inches deep when filled. It is drawn down in mid-April. It is irrigated by tailwater and subirrigation from adjacent irrigated pasture, and grows a mixed stand of swamp timothy, watergrass and smartweed. The unit is flooded up in late September or early October and the

Figure 8 Refuge Management Units

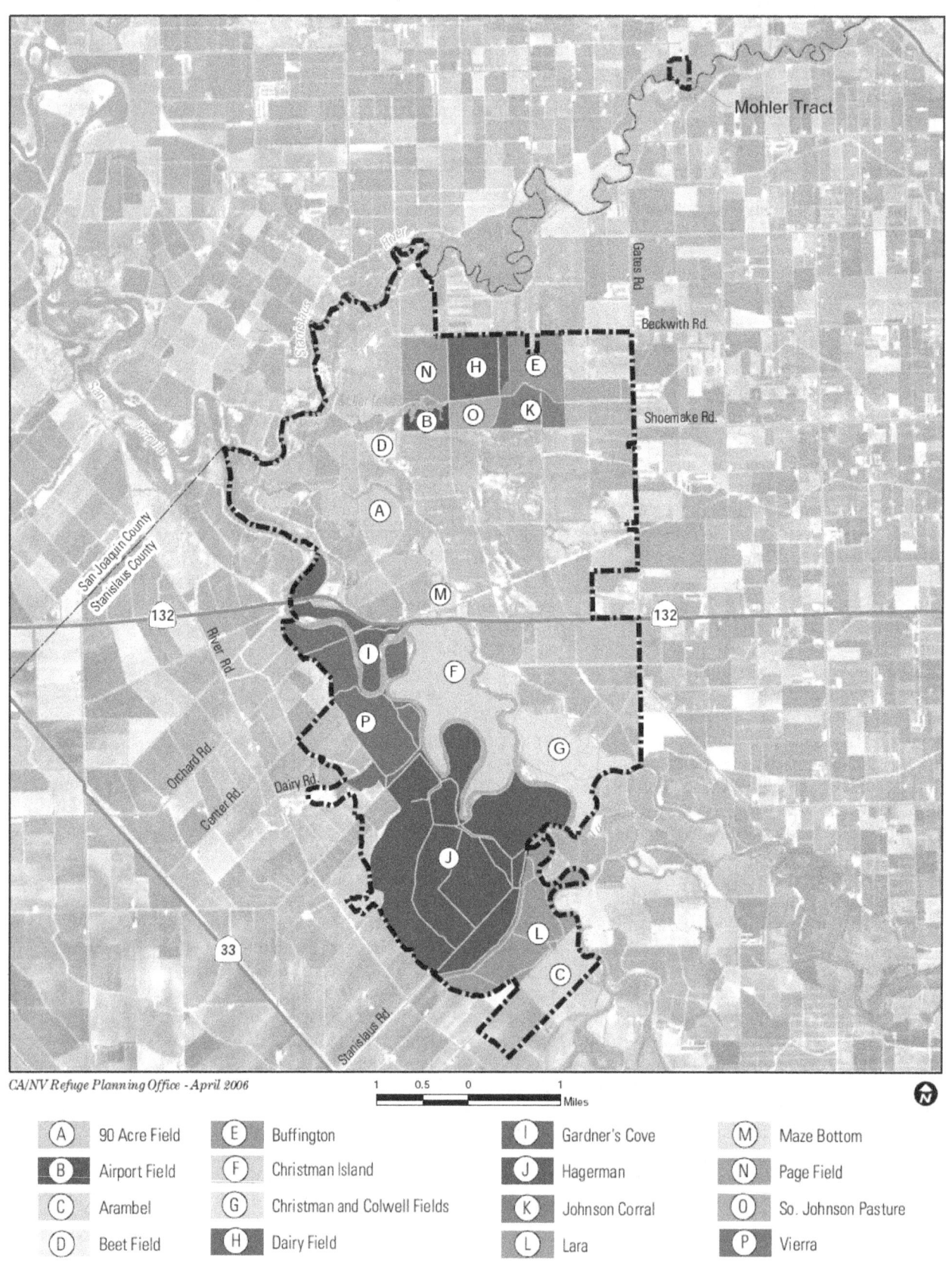

CA/NV Refuge Planning Office - April 2006

A	90 Acre Field	E	Buffington	I	Gardner's Cove	M	Maze Bottom
B	Airport Field	F	Christman Island	J	Hagerman	N	Page Field
C	Arambel	G	Christman and Colwell Fields	K	Johnson Corral	O	So. Johnson Pasture
D	Beet Field	H	Dairy Field	L	Lara	P	Vierra

water level maintained through the winter. The cattail-lined East Nelson Lake is used throughout the year by waterfowl, marsh nesting birds and other wetland dependent wildlife. West Nelson Lake is primarily used as a roost site by Aleutian Canada geese during autumn, but is heavily used from fall through spring by white-fronted geese (*Anser albifrons frontalis*), ducks, sandhill cranes, wading birds and shorebirds.

Ringneck Pond
This wetland unit consists of a permanent cattail-dominated wetland adjacent to a Modesto Irrigation District canal and a meandering seasonal channel extending from the wetland across native uplands. The Modesto Irrigation District Canal supplies water to the unit. Management capabilities are extremely limited due to the poor condition of the water control structure and limited operating season of the Modesto Irrigation District canal system. Within that limitation, the management regime is to flood-up the seasonal channel in November and maintain levels until May. The area is heavily used by sandhill cranes, ducks, wading birds and shorebirds, and is minimally used by geese.

White Lakes
Upper and Lower White lakes are the remnants of a larger White Lake complex that was drained and converted to agricultural fields in the early 1900s. Upper White Lake is supported by a high water table which is supplemented by upslope drainage from off-refuge lands. It is maintained as a permanent wetland and its management flexibility is limited. Prior to Service acquisition, Lower White Lake was recently agricultural cropland bisected by a series of ditches that conveyed drainwater from upslope agricultural fields to the San Joaquin River. The Service is required by law to allow surface tailwater to continue draining across the Refuge. In spring 2000, Refuge staff allowed these drain flows to recreate part of Lower White Lake by restricting flows at the drainage outlet and letting water back into lower portions of the former fields. Within one growing season,

scattered clumps of cattail and roundstem bulrush vegetated the area, which was being used by waterfowl, pelicans, cormorants, wading birds, marsh-nesting birds and other wetland-dependent wildlife. White Lake is currently managed as a permanent wetland, but Refuge staff has the ability to alter wetland regimes by controlling flows from the outlet structure. Monitoring was, and continues to be, conducted to ensure that water levels remain lower that the upslope field drains and do not impact drainage of adjacent private lands. There is an opportunity to expand the size of Lower White Lake by recontouring the former wetland basins and installing additional water control structures.

San Joaquin River Oxbows, Creeks and Sloughs
The Refuge staff has little-to-no control over water levels in the sloughs, creeks and oxbows that are present on the Refuge. Riley Slough meanders across the Mapes Ranch, Refuge lands and the Faith Ranch, and ultimately drains into the San Joaquin River. It is maintained by groundwater and surface tailwater from adjacent irrigated pastures and fields and has highly variable water levels. The Refuge portion of the slough is heavily vegetated by cattails and roundstem bulrush. It is used by ducks, grebes, marsh nesting birds, beaver, western pond turtles (Clemmys marmorota) and other wetland-dependent wildlife. The channelized Hospital Creek, on the west side of the Refuge, conveys agricultural drainwater from upslope sources to the San Joaquin River. The Service is required by law to allow continued drainage of this surface tailwater flow across Refuge lands. Water levels in Hospital Creek are variable. A narrow oxbow (former main channel of the San Joaquin River) extends from the San Joaquin River and forms the west side of Christman Island. The north end of the oxbow is connected to the river, while the south end is connected only during high water. It is maintained by river flows, groundwater and drainage from Hospital Creek. The oxbow and associated plant community supports ducks, cormorants, herons, egrets, riparian associated

songbirds, western pond turtles and other wetland dependent wildlife.

Vernal Pools
Vernal pools are managed by strictly protecting the sites and avoiding any earthmoving activities or other development on native uplands. Seasonal cattle grazing is used to manage for short grass and native forb communities associated with vernal pools.

Upland Management
Current management of upland habitats includes cattle and sheep grazing by cooperators, sharecropping and custom farming, invasive weed control, prescribed burning and floodplain riparian restoration by staff, cooperators and contractors (Figure 5. Refuge Management Unit Map).

Irrigated Pasture and Native Grasslands
Refuge pastures and native grasslands are grazed by cattle through a long-standing CLMA with the Lyons family to provide short grass foraging habitat for Aleutian Canada geese, other geese, sandhill cranes, long-billed curlew (*Numenius americanus*), white-faced ibis (*Plegadis chihi*) and mountain plover (*Charadrius montanus*). In consultation with the grazing cooperator, the Refuge develops annual grazing plans to produce the desired habitat conditions and maintain the long-term viability of pastures and native grassland communities. The irrigated pastures are under a year round grazing regime where cattle are rotated so individual pastures are grazed eight out of 12 months. Native grasslands are grazed seasonally from December 1 through May 15. Due to the size of these grasslands, cattle are moved off and on individual units to avoid overgrazing. In wet springs, grazing may be extended to June 15 to control nonnative invasive weeds. Under terms of the CLMA, grazing fees owed to the Service by the Cooperator are exchanged for an equivalent value in pumping costs to provide water for wetlands, and the production of winter wheat for goose and crane forage on Refuge lands.

Croplands
Corn, winter wheat and alfalfa are grown on Refuge lands to provide winter forage supplies for geese, sandhill cranes and other migratory birds. On the east side of the San Joaquin River (East Unit), approximately 335 acres of corn (Page and Dairy Fields) are grown on a sharecrop basis. The cooperator (Lyons family) harvests his share as silage in September and continues to grow the Refuge share to full maturity as grain corn. The Refuge share of the corn is later mowed by Refuge staff in December or January to provide forage for geese and sandhill cranes. The acreage on which the cooperator's share of corn was grown is disked down and planted to winter wheat in October for the Refuge. Irrigation dates for the wheat are timed to provide a suitable forage height (three to six inches) for geese arriving in October and November.

Forage crops are grown on the west side of the San Joaquin River (West Unit) to promote goose and sandhill crane use on the more recently acquired lands. A 130-acre alfalfa field, which was present prior to the Service acquiring the land in 2000, is being maintained by a cooperator via a CLMA. The management objective for this unit is not only to provide goose and crane habitat in the winter, but also year round foraging habitat for white-faced ibis and long-billed curlew. CLMA revenues owed to the Service are used to pay for Refuge infrastructure repair, water pumping costs and producing winter wheat. Approximately 100 acres of winter wheat are planted each fall as foraging habitat for geese and cranes.

Fallow Agricultural Fields
Guided by this CCP, Refuge staff will restore the fallow agricultural fields to a mosaic of forested riparian and wetland habitats in much of the Refuge land in the floodplain west of the San Joaquin River. Interim management objectives for these lands are to limit the spread of introduced noxious weeds and provide short vegetation winter foraging areas for geese, sandhill cranes and other migratory birds. This is accomplished through mowing and prescribed burning by Refuge staff, and sheep grazing by a cooperator via a CLMA.

Riparian Forest Management
Little or no active habitat manipulation occurs within the Refuge's riparian habitats. Cattle are excluded from riparian corridors to allow understory and mid-story vegetation to be grown in areas that were grazed prior to acquisition.

Invasive Weed Control
The Refuge uses an integrated approach using herbicide application, mowing, prescribed burning, and grazing to control invasive weeds. The amount of weed control to date has been limited due to staffing constraints. Past efforts have focused on herbicide application and mowing to control yellow star thistle on native grasslands on the East Unit and roadside corridors on the West Unit. Removing and foliar spraying of giant reed in the riparian corridor of the West Unit started in summer 2000 and is ongoing.

Habitat Restoration
Recent land acquisition at the Refuge particularly in the western portion consists of fallow agricultural lands. A key element for Refuge management during the next 15 years will be the restoration of these lands.

Wetland Restoration
The Refuge has been funded, through the CALFED program, to restore 300 acres of wetland habitat in the West Unit. A restoration plan has been approved. Engineering design and construction will be initiated in the next few years.

Riparian Restoration
Much of the riparian restoration to date has been passive. Cottonwood, willow, valley oak and other species have become established on portions of the floodplain in recent years after floods and other high water events. Refuge staff and volunteers have also planted cottonwood, valley oak, California rose, box elder and other riparian plant species at Gardner's Cove and the Christmas Island area in 1997 and 1999. The Refuge has been funded, through the CALFED program, to restore 800 acres of riparian floodplain in the West Unit. A reforestation plan has been developed and

a nursery was established on the Refuge in spring 2000 to supply cuttings for that reforestation effort. Planting and growing native trees, shrubs, forbs and grasses began in the winter/spring 2002 through a contract with Sacramento River Partners.

Wildlife Management and Monitoring
Wildlife management and biological monitoring activities to date have been conducted through the Aleutian Canada Goose Recovery Program, special projects funding and grants. Operational biological monitoring has been limited due to staff constraints, and focused on endangered species, flyway and state-wide surveys and avian disease management.

Baseline information on migratory birds, mammals, fish, amphibians, reptiles and vernal pool invertebrates on the Refuge has been expanded through a biological inventory conducted as part of a CALFED habitat acquisition and restoration grant (Phase 1). Biological monitoring will be expanded through funding provided in a current CALFED grant (Phase 2). Data collected would be used to compare long-term wildlife population and habitat use trends as Refuge lands are restored and subsequently managed.

Avian Disease Control
The Refuge staff monitors roost ponds regularly during the winter for bird carcasses or birds displaying disease symptoms. Disease management activities follow the protocols established in the San Luis Complex/Grasslands Management Area Disease Contingency Plan (FWS 1991) and the Aleutian Canada Goose Disease and Contaminant Hazard Contingency Plan (FWS 1987). Mortality and morbidity from avian diseases is common in the Central Valley of California.

Low-level chronic die offs are ordinary, while large avian epidemics are rare. Generally, disease outbreaks occur seasonally in relation to high densities of waterbirds and extreme hot or cold weather conditions. In recent years, avian cholera has been the primary concern for refuge disease managers; however, other important diseases include avian botulism, fungal infections, lead poisoning and chemical toxin poisoning.

Most disease control activities at the Refuge involve avian cholera and are concentrated around goose roost ponds. Avian cholera is a highly contagious bacterial disease that causes the greatest amount of mortality and morbidity in mid to late-winter when waterfowl are concentrated and daily temperatures remain below 10 degrees Celsius. Annual Refuge die-offs range from <50 to >1,200 per year. Beginning in November, the Refuge staff makes regular visits to roost ponds searching for carcasses or birds displaying disease symptoms. All recovered birds are removed from the site and either buried or shipped to the National Wildlife Health Research Center to confirm cause of death. Once an outbreak occurs, daily bird pick-up and disposal is initiated to limit the spread of pathogens to uninfected birds. Under severe epidemics, hazing of waterfowl is initiated to disperse populations and reduce the likelihood of disease transmission. Avian botulism, another disease more common in the southern end of the Central Valley, is uncommon in the northern San Joaquin Valley and has never been recorded at the Refuge. Control activities and documented losses are summarized in annual disease management reports.

Aleutian Canada Goose Monitoring

Refuge staff monitor abundance and habitat use of Aleutian Canada geese to assess response to habitat management actions, document deaths and address crop depredation complaints. In joint operation with the CDFG personnel, refuge staff and volunteers conduct rocket-netting each December to band and neck-collar geese. As funding allows, intensive neck collar observations are made during winter to determine annual population levels and survival rates as outlined in the Pacific Flyway Aleutian Canada Goose Management Plan and meet Service Endangered Species Act obligations for post delisting monitoring.

Riparian Brush Rabbit Reintroduction

The Refuge staff participates with other Federal, State and university personnel in an interagency working group to plan and implement recovery actions for the federally listed endangered riparian brush rabbit. A reintroduction of riparian brush rabbits onto Refuge lands was initiated in the summer of 2002. An elevated mound, to be used as an island refugium by the endangered rabbits during floods, was built and planted to vegetation in the summer of 2001.

Other Migratory Bird Monitoring

Waterfowl
The Refuge staff participates in flyway and state-wide surveys by conducting ground counts to determine species and subspecies flock composition in the November dark goose surveys, periodic white goose surveys, annual midwinter waterfowl surveys and other special surveys. Refuge specific surveys are generally limited to nonsystematic observations to document use of restored and managed habitat. To promote nesting by wood ducks and other cavity nesting birds, nest boxes are maintained by Refuge staff and volunteers. Nest production data is forwarded to the California Waterfowl Association's Wood Duck Program for inclusion in a state-wide database.

Sandhill Cranes
The Refuge staff participates in flyway-wide greater sandhill crane surveys in October. Refuge-specific counts are conducted periodically to document sandhill crane use and abundance on restored and managed habitats.

Shorebirds
Refuge specific surveys are generally limited to nonsystematic observations to document species occurrence and abundance on restored and managed habitat.

Neotropical Migratory Land Birds
The Refuge, jointly with the Point Reyes Bird Observatory, has completed a three year study (2000 to 2002) of avian distribution, abundance, and productivity on Refuge riparian and floodplain habitats.

A permanent MAPS (Monitoring Avian Productivity and Survival) station has been established on the Refuge.

Heron and Egret Rookeries
Counts are conducted each spring to determine the status and abundance of great blue herons and great egrets nesting at traditional rookery sites on Christman Island.

Vernal Pool Fauna Monitoring
Fauna associated with vernal pools are periodically surveyed. Sampling is done on a presence/absence basis rather than more intensive quantitative methods, to avoid impacting populations of federally-listed vernal pool fairy shrimp species and vernal pool tadpole shrimp.

CALFED Restoration Monitoring
A multiyear biological monitoring program was initiated in the autumn of 2001 by Refuge staff and contractors as part of the current CALFED habitat restoration grant (Phase 2). Elements of the monitoring program include migratory bird use of riparian, floodplain and wetland habitats; success of riparian brush rabbit reintroduction efforts; survival of native tree and shrub plantings; development of shaded riverine aquatic habitat; effectiveness of natural versus cultivated riparian restoration; and floodplain habitat changes that result from levee breeching. Depending on a request to amend the CALFED proposal, the monitoring would be expanded to inventory anadromous fish populations; monitor hydrological/fluvial processes following floodplain restoration; determine the status of the endangered species (giant garter snake) and valley elderberry longhorn beetle; and inventory primary pollinator (native bee) populations.

Fire Management
One large wildfire (>500 acres) on Refuge lands occurs on average once every five years and several firestarts usually caused by trespassers occur each year. The borders of interior roads are usually mowed during early summer to reduce the occurrence and spread of any wildfire. The Refuge lands west of the San Joaquin River, due to their relative isolation and fuel type, pose the greatest risk for wildfire. Wildfire suppression capability is primarily provided through the San Luis NWR Complex fire crews and other fire-trained Refuge staff as detailed in the Complex-wide Wildlands Fire Management Plan. The Service also has a signed Memorandum of Understanding with the West Stanislaus County Fire Protection District to provide mutual firefighting support. If necessary, additional firefighting support from other Federal, State, and county agencies can be deployed through the State of California Master Mutual Aid Agreement.

Prescribed fire has been used by the Refuge in an effort to control weeds and prepare lands for restoration work. Plans call for the continued use of fire for site preparation/ habitat maintenance, where it is determined to be the most beneficial and/or cost efficient way to produce desired results. Since 1999, prescribed burning has been used on 300 to 500 acres annually at the Refuge.

Public Use Program
The Refuge has been closed to all public uses since its establishment. This CCP will provide guidance for the future visitor services of the Refuge. Limited public access has been made available for an observation platform, special events and tours led by Refuge staff. Occasional tours are also provided by the Modesto Rotary Club on the Faith Ranch.

Law Enforcement and Public Safety
Law enforcement patrol and surveillance is conducted primarily by the San Luis Complex law enforcement officer and/or collateral-duty officers. Most problems encountered on the Refuge involve trespass into closed areas, illegal fishing, littering, marijuana cultivation, other drug-related activities, campfires and violation of Migratory Bird Treaty and Endangered Species Act regulations. Additional support is provided as necessary by Service Special Agents, CDFG wardens and other law enforcement agencies.

4 Opportunities and Problems

All National Wildlife Refuges possess inherent distinctive characteristics and infrastructure which influence and impact management of the Refuge's resources. These refuge-specific attributes at times can be challenges, needs and/or opportunities and can augment, enhance, diminish or facilitate the management of natural resources at a National Wildlife Refuge. In order to meet management goals and planning requirements, these challenges, opportunities, restrictions and needs of the Refuge must be identified and addressed. The following list contains attributes and characteristics of the San Joaquin River NWR which present either opportunities, needs and/or challenges to the management of the Refuge and which need to be considered for this planning process.

Water Quantity and Quality

Supplies

Lack of a reliable water supply is a critical problem for this Refuge. Water is needed for management of wetland habitats, as well as for management of some upland habitats and riparian woodland restoration activities. Unlike most Central Valley National Wildlife Refuges, the San Joaquin River NWR does not receive a water allocation from the Bureau of Reclamation under the authority of the Central Valley Project Improvement Act. Only a small portion of the San Joaquin River NWR is within the Modesto Irrigation District and use of that water is restricted to their service area. Water used for Refuge management east of the San Joaquin River has been provided by the privately-owned Mapes Ranch as value due to the Service through their CLMA, as tailwater from adjacent grazing/farming operations or as water in excess of their needs. This CLMA does not generate

enough fees to cover the cost of providing water. Supply of free tailwater and excess water will likely be limited in the future due to water conservation measures and potential water marketing. The availability of water from existing lift pumps on Refuge lands recently acquired by the Service is restricted due to limited resources, funding and other constraints. Service-owned wells, which could meet some water supply needs, are present on the Refuge but funds for their operation are lacking. The water supply available to the Refuge will impact the management of both upland and wetland habitats.

Infrastructure

Water production and associated delivery systems on Refuge lands are either in poor or in flood-damaged condition. Of the six lift pumps along the San Joaquin (five) and the Tuolumne (one) rivers, five need to be rehabilitated to make them operational and upgraded to meet OSHA safety standards, and all need fish screens installed to preclude impacts to threatened and endangered fish. The Service-owned canals and other water conveyance systems need to be repaired and in some cases, realigned to more efficiently deliver water to Refuge habitats. In addition, water used to manage lands east of the San Joaquin River must be transported across lands and through delivery systems owned by private owners. An alternate delivery system or formal conveyance agreements need to be developed and completed to ensure the long-term ability to provide water to the Refuge's habitats.

Contaminants

The San Joaquin River is designated as an impaired waterway by the U.S. Environmental Protection Agency. Although water quality is generally acceptable, there are times of the year when this water should not be applied to Refuge wetlands due to potential long-term impacts to wildlife and habitat. Regional mandates associated with managing salt, boron, dissolved oxygen and selenium levels/loads may in future years restrict the ability of the Service to use its water rights to manage Refuge lands.

Surface drainage and tailwater are also used from upslope agricultural operations to manage part of the Refuge's wetlands. The Refuge needs to ascertain if the quality of this water is acceptable for use in managing wetlands or whether it should be conveyed directly through the Refuge only to meet the legal drainage requirements for adjacent lands.

Water Rights and Other Rights

Water is a critical element for management of the majority of lands in the Central Valley, including the management of wildlife on wildlands. Because of the high cost of water in the Central Valley, wetland management for wildlife on a per acre basis in the Central Valley is probably the highest in the nation (Heitmeyer et al. 1989). Access to water, as well as its quantity and quality, will impact land management activities. Water rights and agreements associated with land will influence and constrain natural resource management planning and decisions at the San Joaquin River NWR. The following sections detail these rights for Refuge lands.

Water Rights

The availability and cost of water will impact the planned wildlife management programs which could occur at the San Joaquin River NWR. The State Water Resources Control Board conducted a review to determine the water rights associated with the San Joaquin River NWR. The State of California recognizes both appropriative and riparian water rights. The use of water for a beneficial purpose establishes an appropriative water right that must be accompanied by a water use permit issued by the State. A riparian water right is established by ownership of land abutting a natural water course. The review indicated

that there are two appropriative and one riparian water right. These three water rights supplied water to a portion of the lands purchased from the El Solyo Dairy, Ed Hagemann and J. P. Lara (Rausch 1999). There are also one appropriative and three riparian water rights on lands within the approved Refuge boundary that are not owned by the Service. This inquiry did not detail water rights with points of diversion outside the area considered (for example, the Modesto Irrigation District water right which serves the western portions of the Refuge, but the point of diversion is outside the vicinity of the Refuge).

Drainage (White Lake Mutual Water Company)

This agreement maintains that the West Stanislaus Irrigation District has drainage rights over land purchased from Hagemann (Mehlhaff and Hay, 1999), now Service-owned land, which arise from a drainage reservation easement in the 1941 deed conveying the land from Burkhard Investment Company to Hagemann's predecessor (Mr. Pietro Rampion). The agreement protects those lands against seepage from the District's canal, except those lands outside of the District. West Stanislaus Irrigation District obtained a Memorandum of Agreement on May 8, 1928 with Burkhard Investment Company, which was later amended in 1939. The agreement addresses the right of access and construction for the White Lake Mutual Water Company intake channel, as well as the obligation to protect the Refuge land from canal seepage.

In addition, the White Lake Mutual Water Company pays 35 percent of drainage facility maintenance and pumping costs for the drainage ditch system over land purchased from Hagemann (Mehlhaff and Hay 1999). White Lake Mutual Water Company also has an obligation to operate drainage pumps on Refuge property purchased from J. P. Lara. The 1928 agreement requires the landowner (now the Service) to "maintain the water level and seepage from the main canal at 22 U.S.E.D. and at least eight feet below the natural, average ground level, the district to install, maintain the necessary pumps and operate the pumping of the seepage water." Access across the White Lake Mutual Water Company canal was previously provided by three pile bridges, which are now unusable.

Rights-of Way

White Lake Mutual Water Company Right of Way
This agreement grants "free ingress, egress and regress" to White Lake Mutual Water Company and the "use of a strip of land thirty feet wide along the natural channel of Hospital Creek" extending from the existing creek crossing along the main river levee to the confluence with the San Joaquin River for "drainage ditch and road purposes." The White Lake Mutual Water Company shall, at its own cost, maintain 20 cubic feet per second (cfs) capacity and replace the culvert when necessary.

Hetch Hetchy Aqueduct Right of Way
The January 2, 1924 agreement between the Central-California Orchard Company (Grantor) and the City and County of San Francisco, a municipal corporation, to "grant, bargain and sell" parcel 1 and 2 (as described in the indenture) to the "Grantee and to its successors (Service) assigns forever" upon which the center line of the two parcels is a part of the center line of the Hetch Hetchy Aqueduct right of way. The City and County of San Francisco own "all the lands of Grantor included within a strip of land 110 feet in width" along the aqueduct corridor (certain reservations and conditions are outlined in the official document). Easements also exist on Parcel 1 and 2 for three canals. Parcel 1 includes an easement for road purposes and Parcel 2 includes an easement for single pole transmission lines, conveyed to the Pacific Gas and Electric Company.

Floodplain and Riparian Restoration
The majority of Refuge lands west of the San Joaquin River are abandoned agricultural fields that currently provide little benefit to riparian and wetland dependent wildlife species. A major Refuge initiative and need is to restore

natural habitats for wildlife. A project to restore wetland and riparian habitats on approximately one-third of these lands has been funded and planning has been initiated. Additional habitat restoration funding is needed to restore the remaining floodplain to maximize benefits to riparian and wetland dependent species.

Grassland Communities
Central Valley grassland habitats have been severely altered over the past 150 years. Exotic annual grasses, principally of Mediterranean origin, replaced the valley's native perennial grasses, which probably dominated these grasslands. Restoration of native habitats is a critical element of Refuge management. Typically, techniques for restoring native Central Valley grasslands have not been successful on a large scale, or have been too costly. To reestablish native grasslands at the Refuge, successful methods based on reasonable costs will need to be adopted and/or developed.

Invasive Weeds & Other Exotic Species
Invasive weeds are non-native plants which have the capacity to invade and dominate a plant community. These invasive weeds frequently reduce the quality of the habitat to wildlife, are extremely costly to eradicate, resist control efforts and are a major source of concern for many natural resource managers in many regions.

Non-native plants dominate major portions of the Central Valley landscape. Serious pest plants occurring in the Refuge's uplands include yellow star thistle, perennial pepperweed, poison hemlock, Russian thistle, milk thistle, bull thistle and prickly lettuce. Infestations are greatest in fallow agricultural fields, roadsides, canal banks, and undergrazed pastures, as well as other disturbed sites. Efforts to control thistles need to be addressed within managed pastures, especially those undergoing rehabilitation. Control of these invasive weeds will improve the quality of upland wildlife habitat at the Refuge.

A major effort is also required to control invasive weeds in areas being restored to natural riparian and wetland habitats.

Perennial pepperweed is established throughout the Refuge's riparian areas and stands of arundo are scattered along the banks of the San Joaquin River. These invasive plants, if left untreated, will crowd native plants and eventually dominate the riparian corridor, reducing the quality of the habitat for wildlife. Efforts need to be greatly expanded to control perennial pepperweed and ensure the eradication of arundo. At certain times of the year, the San Joaquin River can be heavily infested with water hyacinth. These floating plants have a rapid growth rate and high reproductive capabilities, which lead to clogged water delivery canals and impenetrable surfaces covering oxbows and other wetlands. Physical barriers and other control measures need to be established to ensure that hyacinth is not transported to Refuge wetland habitats.

The black rat is another invasive species that may be impacting the Refuge. Originally restricted to Europe and Asia, this species has colonized portions of North America. In California, the black rat is found in the Central Valley and coastal areas. Its preferred habitat is urban areas and stream courses (i.e., riparian habitat). The black rat is considered to have a negative impact on the endangered San Joaquin Valley woodrat. Although the black rat is known to occur at the Refuge, its abundance and impact on native fauna and flora is not known. Control programs regarding the black rat may become necessary if research indicates the woodrat or other indigenous species are severely impacted by this species.

Threatened and Endangered Species

Threatened and endangered species are wildlife and plants designated by the Service as species whose population or local population is in danger of extirpation. The management of threatened and endangered species is a priority for the Service's National Wildlife Refuge System. The San Joaquin River NWR supports and has the potential to benefit a number of these rare species. Programs conducted at the Refuge for threatened and endangered species can also set limits on other activities at the Refuge.

Riparian Brush Rabbit

This endangered rabbit remains in only four known locales -- one of which is the San Joaquin River NWR. The riparian brush rabbit's decline is largely attributed to the loss of riparian forest in the Central Valley. The Refuge has the potential to significantly increase the population of this endangered species due to its present riparian forested habitats and plans for the restoration of additional riparian forest. Management for the riparian brush rabbit will require that the Refuge protect, manage and restore riparian habitats.

San Joaquin Valley Woodrat

The presence of the San Joaquin Valley woodrat requires that it become a management priority. Similar to the riparian brush rabbit, the endangered San Joaquin Valley woodrat requires riparian forest as habitat, and in particular, an overstory of oak with a dense woody understory. The loss of riparian forest within the San Joaquin Valley has led a decline in this species. This endangered woodrat has been documented at the San Joaquin River NWR; however, no systematic surveys have been conducted. Initially, the Refuge needs to determine this species' current distribution and abundance; future plans will depend on the outcome of this survey work.

San Joaquin Kit Fox

The endangered San Joaquin Kit Fox is the smallest canid in North America. Its habitat includes arid grasslands in the southern half of the Central Valley. No sightings of kit fox have been documented at the San Joaquin River NWR and the fox's preferred habitat is scarce at the Refuge. The kit fox is known to occur directly to the west of the Refuge. The Complex will monitor the Refuge for kit fox use and, depending on its presence, modify its management programs, as needed, for the species.

Bald Eagle

The threatened bald eagle is a sporadic winter visitor to the San Joaquin River NWR. It tends to be attracted to waterfowl concentrations on the Refuge. Eagles are largely absent from the Refuge during the breeding season. Wetland restoration efforts will likely benefit this species.

Aleutian Canada Geese
Although the Aleutian Canada goose was delisted as a Federal Threatened Species in March 2001, it remains a Service Species of Special Concern. The Endangered Species Act mandates that populations of recovered species be monitored for five years post-delisting to ensure that recovery goals continue to be met. The long-standing monitoring program at the Refuge needs to continue to comply with the law and document whether Aleutian Canada goose numbers remain stable, increase or decrease. This is part of a larger monitoring program and cannot be sustained with existing Refuge funds. Specific project funds are needed to implement this monitoring. In addition, on-refuge monitoring is necessary to evaluate use of Refuge habitat and address localized crop depredation complaints from nearby landowners.

Least Bell's Vireo
This federally-designated endangered songbird was documented as breeding for the first time at the Refuge in 2005. It used as breeding habitat, a unit with restored riparian habitat. Although once a common breeder in the Central Valley, least Bell's vireo during the last few decades has been confined to southern California. Plans to restore significant tracts of riparian habitat at the Refuge will likely provide additional habitat for this species and the Refuge will need to monitor for the presence and abundance of this species during the next fifteen years.

Giant Garter Snake
The status of the federally-designated endangered giant garter snake at the San Joaquin River NWR is unknown. No systematic surveys have been conducted for this species, although the Refuge appears to contain suitable habitat. The Refuge needs to conduct surveys to determine if the giant garter snake is present and, if so, at what locations and habitats so that appropriate protective measures can be taken.

Anadromous and Other Listed Fish Species
Chinook salmon, Sacramento splittail, and potentially, steelhead trout can be impacted by Refuge management. Fish screens need to be installed on the Refuge lift pumps along the San Joaquin and Tuolumne rivers to ensure that juvenile fish are not negatively affected by pump operation. The design for levee breeching and floodplain restoration at the Refuge needs to be closely coordinated with fisheries biologists to avoid creating conditions that promote fish entrapment (Appendix H: Levee Breach).

Because salmon and splittail fry would probably use the floodplain wetlands during high-water or flood years, wetland management must limit populations of predatory non-native fish. Through design and management, the floodplain wetlands have the potential to benefit Chinook salmon and Sacramento splittail populations by providing high quality rearing habitat.

Valley Elderberry Longhorn Beetle
To date, there has been little effort to document the presence of the valley elderberry longhorn beetle at the Refuge or to inventory elderberry locations, the only habitat it uses. It is necessary to increase knowledge of the actual and potential distribution of this species on the Refuge to ensure that ongoing and future restoration incorporates its habitat needs and subsequent management contributes to species recovery.

Vernal Pool Invertebrate Species
Two federally-listed vernal pool invertebrates (i.e., vernal pool fairy shrimp and vernal pool tadpole shrimp) occur at the San Joaquin River NWR. Protection of vernal pool habitats at the Refuge needs to be established and rigorously enforced. Protocols for monitoring these invertebrates and their habitats also need to be developed and implemented.

State-Listed Species
The State of California has also developed its own list of threatened and endangered species. The species addressed in the

preceding descriptions are federally designated threatened/endangered species, although many of these are also listed by the State. State-listed species known to occur or with the potential to occur at the San Joaquin River NWR include the greater sandhill crane, yellow-billed cuckoo, Swainson's hawk, willow flycatcher and bank swallow. As a first step, the Refuge needs to determine the distribution and abundance of these species on the San Joaquin River NWR; then, the Refuge should develop and implement management plans for each species that is present.

Fire

Wildfire is a natural process in most terrestrial systems. Wildfires are a major ecological process impacting vegetative succession and structure in many regions. Many species of plants and wildlife are adapted to fire disturbance. Climate, terrain, vegetation and drainage all influence the role and timing of wildfire occurrence and impacts. Some areas have short interval wildfire regimes, while others have extremely long interval wildfire regimes (greater than 500 years). Typically, grassland-dominated areas have short interval fire regimes and many species of grass are well adapted and suited to wildfire disturbance.

However, grassland habitats in California's Central Valley, including the Refuge, have been severely altered over the past 150 years. Exotic annual grass species principally of Mediterranean origin replaced native perennial grasses that likely dominated these grasslands.. Although there is some thought that the original fire regime in the Central Valley was a short-time interval, there is little information available to land managers regarding suitable time intervals and seasonal timing for the use of fire in maintaining or restoring native grasslands, as well as other Central Valley native habitats. The Refuge will face challenges in determining suitable fire regime intervals and seasonal timing for the application of fire in terrestrial habitats, restoring native grasslands from exotic annual-dominated grasslands, and

implementing a prescribed fire program to mimic a natural ecological process in an area with air quality problems.

Mosquito Abatement

Issues concerning mosquitoes and their associated problems (i.e., nuisance biting and vector-born diseases) are frequently encountered with aquatic habitats, particularly when they are in proximity to human habitations (*Pratt and Moore 1993*). Aquatic habitats and wetlands, as well as irrigated pasture, provide conditions for breeding mosquitoes on the Refuge. The San Joaquin River NWR is situated within two local mosquito control agencies (Turlock and Eastside Mosquito Abatement Districts). Both are active districts and conduct mosquito monitoring programs (both larvae and adults), as well as disease monitoring programs (i.e., encephalitis, malaria and West Nile Fever) on the Refuge. Both districts also conduct larvaciding programs on the Refuge with the approval of the Refuge Manager and when conditions warrant. Control programs for adult mosquitoes are not permitted on the Refuge unless there is a declared public health emergency. In the past 15 years, only one public health emergency has been declared concerning a mosquito-born disease at the San Joaquin River NWR or its vicinity. Mosquito abatement on Refuge lands will require that the USFWS ensures that mosquito programs do not negatively impact natural resources and addresses legitimate mosquito nuisance and disease issues in neighboring communities.

Public Use Programs

Public use programs can be extremely beneficial in promoting wildlife and National Wildlife Refuges, establishing community involvement with the Refuge, creating cooperative partnerships to benefit wildlife, offering environmental educational opportunities and providing wildlife-dependent recreational opportunities for the public. The San Joaquin River NWR has never been opened to public use, with the exception of a recently-established roadside wildlife observation platform.

Opening the Refuge to the public offers a major opportunity and challenge. This will require developing and implementing a step-down public use plan for the Refuge that will outline which activities will occur, where they will occur, and what precautions are needed to assure that the public use program does not negatively impact the wildlife resource. National Wildlife Refuges have public use programs to allow for the enjoyment of our nation's fish and wildlife resources. The Improvement Act for the National Wildlife Refuge System identified wildlife as the principal management goal of all Refuges. If the Refuge can accommodate a public use program, the Act indicates it should focus on six wildlife-dependent public uses—wildlife viewing, photography, hunting, fishing, environmental education and nature interpretation.

Law Enforcement

During its first 15 years, there has been no staff permanently stationed at the Refuge. As a result, a strong Service presence has been lacking and trespass has routinely occurred, as well as other illegal activities, such as all terrain vehicle use, dumping, marijuana cultivation and vandalism. To rectify this situation, over the past two years USFWS personnel have been permanently stationed at the San Joaquin River NWR. Additional measures are still required to protect Refuge natural resources and assure public safety, including increased public contact, patrols, interagency cooperation and coordination, boundary posting and signage.

Cultural Resources

The Central Valley has a rich Native American cultural history. The cultural resources on the San Joaquin River NWR have not been determined or mapped, even though most of the present Refuge lands were previously disturbed (principally for agricultural activities) by former landowners. Any activity identified in this plan, including land development, grazing, and changes in public use, has the potential to impact cultural resources; however, Federal legislation (National Historic Preservation Act of 1966) protects cultural resources and requires agencies, such as the Service, to consider, and if necessary, mitigate the impacts of its projects on cultural resources before implementation. The Service will comply by consulting with the USFWS Region 1 Cultural Resources Team regarding management activities and programs at the San Joaquin River NWR. The Service is not proposing any project, activity or program that would result in changes in the character of, or would potentially adversely affect, any historic cultural resource or archaeological site.

Refuge Farming Program

Irrigated pastures, which are part of the Refuge's CLMA program, provide critical foraging habitat for Aleutian Canada geese, sandhill cranes, white-faced ibis and other migratory birds. Several of these pastures, especially those north of Highway 132, have not been rehabilitated or rotated for decades. Although the fields are maintained in a short-cropped condition by grazing, the grasses and forbs are decreasing in forage quality for wildlife. Ultimately, wildlife use of the pastures will decline. These pastures need to be rehabilitated by discing under the existing vegetation, reseeding with a mix of grass and forbs and controlling invasive weeds as pastures are established. Refuge funding is currently unavailable to accomplish this work, and the current CLMAs do not generate enough value to allow cooperators to rehabilitate the pastures in exchange for grazing fees owed to the Service. Pasture rehabilitation needs to be pursued through the USFWS Refuge Operating Needs (RONS) process and/or other funding initiatives.

The current practices of sharecrop production of corn and farming of winter wheat on the Refuge provide winter foraging habitat for geese, sandhill cranes, and other migratory birds; however, these practices do not provide any benefits for ground nesting birds during the breeding season. Normally, the wheat field is disced to prepare it for planting corn in the spring. Producing corn by a means other than sharecropping would free the cooperator's share (80 percent) of this acreage, which could be left as a fallow wheat field in the spring and summer.

Such a practice would provide high quality habitat for ground nesting birds such as waterfowl, northern harriers (*Circus cyaneus*), savannah sparrows (*Passerculus sandwichensis*), and other grassland-dependent songbirds. The value of the CLMA grazing at the Refuge is insufficient to pay for the production of corn on a custom farming basis. The farming program will provide limited benefits to ground nesting birds until another mechanism is found to pay for the production of corn, where the Refuge owns all of the crop for use as wildlife forage—thus reducing the acreage needed for planting.

Partnerships

Partnerships are key to the management of National Wildlife Refuges. These partnerships can be with other agencies, private groups and/or individuals and have a focus on accomplishing some aspect of the Refuge's mission. Although the San Joaquin River NWR's direction to date has principally focused on land acquisition, the Refuge has formed significant partnerships for a variety of natural resource management issues and activities. Partnerships are beneficial to the Refuge, not only in accomplishing projects which would not have been possible with limited Refuge staff and funds, but also by expanding public outreach for the Refuge, bringing community input and support into the management process and providing for natural resource management on a landscape scale.

Refuge partnerships have resulted in land acquisition, enhanced programs for endangered/threatened species, natural resource monitoring, and habitat restoration activities, among other projects. Partners involved with the Refuge include local landowners and representatives from the NRCS, California Department of Fish and Game (CDFG), CALFED Bay-Delta Program (CALFED), U.S. Army Corps of Engineers (Corps), Endangered Species Recovery Program, Central Valley Habitat Joint Venture, Tuolumne River Technical Advisory Committee, U.S. Fish and Wildlife Service's Anadromous Fish Restoration Program (AFRP), Bureau of Reclamation (BOR) and Ducks Unlimited, Inc. These existing and potential partnerships for the San Joaquin River NWR will influence planning and management efforts.

Point Reyes Bird Observatory

The Point Reyes Bird Observatory and the San Luis NWR Complex initiated a project in 2000 to monitor songbird use of Refuge lands along the San Joaquin River between the Stanislaus and Tuolumne rivers. A large-scale riparian restoration project planned by the Refuge is in the planning stage and involves 3,300 acres of former agricultural lands within the floodplain. The objective of this partnership is to establish a long-term songbird monitoring program to determine the baseline condition of the bird community, assess bird population responses to the riparian habitat expansion and monitor songbird recolonization and use of restored areas. Prerestoration data on songbird abundance, distribution and reproductive success were collected in existing riparian habitat and in the fallow agricultural fields slated for restoration. Preliminary results from the first year's data indicate the Refuge's potential as an important area for songbirds.

San Joaquin River Resource Management Coalition

The purpose of this organization is "to create a clearly defined, landowner-led organization that partners with nongovernmental organizations and Federal, State and local agencies with diverse interest, mandates and fiscal responsibilities in the San Joaquin River to collaboratively and proactively address resource management challenges and can communicate more effectively across jurisdictional boundaries" *(San Joaquin River Resource Management Coalition Workplan)*. The coalition would work together to increase political understanding, increase awareness of the importance of a balanced healthy river ecosystem, provide a forum to address resource management issues and address current and proposed legislation that affects the San Joaquin River.

Tuolumne River Technical Advisory Committee

The Tuolumne River Technical Advisory Committee (TRTAC) was formed as result of the 1995 Federal Energy Regulatory Commission (FERC) Settlement Agreement for relicensing the new Don Pedro Dam. The group is composed of representatives from Federal, State, and local agencies, non-governmental organizations and interested private parties, and has been directed to coordinate and administer restoration and management activities on the Tuolumne River. The Service participates in the committee and provides funding for projects. The Refuge boundary includes the confluence of the San Joaquin and Tuolumne rivers, and approximately 1.5 shoreline miles of the Tuolumne River. Restoration and management of Refuge riparian habitat contributes to the objectives of the TRTAC, and in turn, upstream actions of TRTAC will improve the ecological health of Refuge lands and assist in attaining -large-scale ecosystem restoration goals of the Service.

CALFED Bay-Delta Program

The CALFED Bay-Delta Program (CALFED) is a collaborative effort among 23 state and federal agencies to improve water supplies in California and the health of the San Francisco Bay-Sacramento-San Joaquin River Delta watershed. It is cooperatively implemented by those signatory agencies through their respective program authorities and pertinent funding mechanisms. Restoration and subsequent management of Refuge lands directly contribute to the goals of CALFED's Ecosystem Restoration Program. CALFED has become a funding partner with the Refuge through issuance of major habitat protection/restoration grants. Since 1997, the Refuge has obtained CALFED grants for land acquisition, habitat restoration and biological inventories/monitoring.

Nonstructural Flood Control Alternative—Corps

The U.S. Army Corps of Engineers, Sacramento Office, has been working to develop a nonstructural flood control alternative on the west side of the Stanislaus River to address flooding problems at and adjacent to the San Joaquin River NWR. The purpose of this project is to replace existing flood control measures via levees with a more natural, resources-friendly alternative. The Corps' proposal is a joint project with the Service to acquire lands for the Refuge protected by the levee; obtain and/or offer easements for areas that were not within the project boundary but received flood protection provided by the freeboard of the project levee; construct ring levees to protect structures and buildings on the Refuge; and work cooperatively to deauthorize the levees and create breeches in the levees to establish a more natural floodplain hydrology on Refuge lands. A joint-agency agreement for this project is in place. The Corps' environmental assessment for this project has also been approved. The Service has already acquired the properties previously protected by the Corps' project levee in accordance with the agreement and the Corps has obtained/offered easements to private landowners whose property is not within the project levee boundary but which received some level of flood protection. The ring levees to protect buildings on the Refuge are scheduled to be constructed the summer of 2004.

Sacramento-San Joaquin River Comprehensive Study—Corps

In response to the January 1997 floods along the Sacramento and San Joaquin rivers, the U.S. Army Corps of Engineers and the California Reclamation Board are preparing the Sacramento and San Joaquin River Basins Comprehensive Study. The study will include a comprehensive master plan for flood damage reduction and ecosystem restoration within the Sacramento River and San Joaquin River basins. Due to the physical, socioeconomic and political complexities, and resource issues within the study area, the master plan will consist of different components and corresponding evaluation of the components. The study will develop broad scale systematic components and the resulting report will present a system-wide analysis of the physical and/or operation changes to the exiting flood control system. Other programmatic components

Refuge partnerships have resulted in land acquisition, enhanced programs for endangered/threatened species, natural resource monitoring, and habitat restoration activities.

could identify new or modified land use management and flood damage reduction programs.

The study first looked at the flood control and environmental problems in the system. Topographic and bathymetric data of the Sacramento and San Joaquin River basins were collected, describing the contour of the existing land surface and river channels to be used in the analysis of hydraulic and environmental effects of potential measures. Using this data, hydrologic and hydraulic models of the Sacramento and San Joaquin Rivers systems were developed. These basin-wide models incorporated historic rainfall-runoff, reservoir operations and flood routing, including unsteady flow along the major river systems. A conceptual plan for an Ecosystems Function Model was developed. In combination with the hydrologic modeling, the Ecosystems Function Model will focus on physical processes that drive biological responses in river systems and floodplains and will be used to evaluate the effects of hydrologic and hydraulic changes on existing and potential aquatic, wetland and riparian habitats.

The comprehensive study is scheduled for completion in the next few years. Complex staff have been interacting with personnel working on the Comprehensive Study to integrate issues involving the San Joaquin River NWR into the process. It is anticipated that the plan would be implemented in stages.

Highway 132 Realignment—Caltrans
The California Department of Transportation (Caltrans) began investigating the possibility of the expansion and/or realignment of Highway 132 before the San Joaquin River NWR was established. Highway 132 is the east-west highway that roughly bisects the Refuge. Although the project has remained inactive for years, recent increases in traffic volume have made these improvements a higher priority. Currently, Caltrans anticipates that an expressway would be constructed within the 15- year planning cycle of this CCP. During the establishment of the Refuge in

1987, the Service issued a formal letter to Caltrans stating that the Service would not oppose expanding Highway 132, but would work with the State agency and others to address and minimize impacts to the Refuge and meet environmental regulations.

Anadromous Fish Restoration Program
The Anadromous Fish Restoration Program was established by the Secretary of Interior through the Central Valley Project Improvement Act, with the mandate to double the natural production of anadromous fish in Central Valley streams. The program is administered by the Service and BOR in cooperation with State agencies, such as CDFG and other partners. The three rivers present on the San Joaquin River NWR make it a key area for this joint program.

Local Landowners
The Refuge has greatly benefited from a long-term partnership with the Bill Lyons Sr. family, owners of the Mapes Ranch; and the Robert Gallo family, owners of the Faith Ranch. The owners of those two ranches have worked with the Service to provide high quality wildlife habitat. While conducting their regular ranching and farming operations, the Gallo and Lyons families have limited disturbance to wildlife on their properties, maintained waterfowl roost ponds and tolerated increasing levels of goose foraging on their pastures and fields. In previous years, the Service contracted with both ranches to grow crops exclusively for waterfowl. Currently, the Service has a cooperative land management agreement (CLMA) and sharecropping agreement with the Lyons family on Refuge lands. The Gallo family, in conjunction with a local Rotary Club and the Service, has implemented a regular tour program on the Faith Ranch and Refuge lands for school groups from Stanislaus County.

Cooperative Land Management Agreement (CLMA)
Since its inception, the San Joaquin River NWR has entered into a number of cooperative land management agreements with members of the community. These

agreements allow a limited agricultural program (i.e., grazing, small grains, etc.) to occur which benefit both specific wildlife resources, as well as the cooperator. The CLMA process is a tool of the Refuge that allows an expanded management program for wildlife, while not depleting limited Refuge staff and funds.

Other Restoration and Management Partners

The San Joaquin River NWR has benefited from the research of many agency and non-agency personnel who have conducted annual Aleutian Canada goose monitoring on site as part of the Aleutian Canada Goose Recovery Program since 1975. Complex and CDFG staffs have jointly banded and neck-collared Aleutian Canada geese at the Refuge annually since 1995. Staff and students of CSU-Stanislaus and Modesto Junior College have assisted Refuge staff in goose banding and other management activities. The Complex staff is working jointly with the Service's Endangered Species Office, BOR, the California State University—Stanislaus Endangered Species Recovery Program and CDFG to re-introduce the riparian brush rabbit onto the Refuge as part of its Recovery Program.

5 Management Goals, Objectives, and Strategies

Introduction

This chapter focuses on the goals, objectives and strategies selected for the management of San Joaquin River NWR. During the preparation of this Comprehensive Conservation Plan, the Service examined and analyzed various management alternatives for the San Joaquin River NWR to best achieve the mission of the National Wildlife Refuge System, Refuge purposes, vision statement and goals; it also considered the existing infrastructure of the Refuge as outlined in Chapters 1 and 3 and the Refuge's resource challenges and needs, listed in Chapter 4. Agencies, non-governmental organizations and the public provided input used to develop the management alternatives. The alternatives were examined for both natural resource management and public use activities at the Refuge. These alternatives were considered and their impacts were reviewed in an environmental assessment (EA) as part of this plan's compliance with the National Environmental Policy Act (Appendix B).

Prior Management Activities at the Refuge

The San Joaquin River NWR was established in 1987 and its original purpose was to provide winter habitat for the then endangered Aleutian Canada goose. Original fee title lands comprising the Refuge included the East Unit parcels and Christman Island. Since Service acquisition, the East Unit lands have been actively managed as winter habitat for the Aleutian Canada goose. In 1996, the Refuge developed a set of interim informal goals to guide Refuge management until a management plan could be developed. These interim goals include the following:

- Provide feeding and resting habitat for wintering waterfowl;

- Provide habitat and manage for endangered, threatened and/or sensitive species of concern;

- Protect and provide habitat for neotropical migratory landbirds;

- Preserve a natural diversity and abundance of plants and animals;

- Provide an area for compatible, wildlife-oriented research; and

- Provide public use activities such as wildlife observation, photography, environmental education, fishing, and hunting.

Although activities were conducted to meet these interim goals on the Refuge, the dominant management activities remained managing winter habitat for the Aleutian Canada goose. Expansion of the existing program was largely precluded due to a shortage of staff and funding, although groundwork was laid for future development of the Refuge's programs. The principle public use activities at the Refuge were wildlife viewing and photography from an observation platform. The only prepared and approved plan for the San Joaquin River Refuge was the Wildland Fire Management Plan, completed by San Luis National Wildlife Refuge Complex in 2001, and a Spill Response Plan, completed in 2003.

Goals, Objectives and Strategies to Support the Proposed Management Action

This section presents long-term guidance for the Refuge in the form of goals, objectives and strategies. Goals guide the future direction of the Refuge. Goals support the Refuge purpose and System mission by providing guidance regarding how the Refuge should operate and what the Refuge should be. Goals represent end results and provide management direction for the

Refuge purposes. Each goal is supported by measurable, achievable objectives, where appropriate; these are the efforts or action items required to achieve the goals. The intent is to accomplish objectives during the duration of this plan; however, actual implementation may vary due to funding and staffing. Objectives, in most cases, provide quantitative benchmarks that indicate progress toward achieving goals. Strategies are specific actions or projects that would lead to the accomplishment of management objectives.

Five broad goals were developed for San Joaquin River NWR. They are consistent with the Refuge purposes, ecoregion goals, National Wildlife Refuge System goals, Refuge Improvement Act, Service policy and international treaties. These goals, objectives and strategies are detailed below. Figure 9 shows the proposed habitat management plan for the Refuge.

Goal 1 (Biological Diversity)

Conserve and protect the natural diversity of migratory birds, resident wildlife, fish and plants through restoration and management of riparian, upland and wetland habitats on Refuge lands.

Foraging white-faced ibis.
Photo: Gary Powell

Narrative: Healthy, high quality habitats are a key to functioning, self-sustaining fish and wildlife communities. Natural conditions that existed during the mid-1800s provide a reference point for comparisons with existing conditions. An assumption is that at this point in time, ecological processes were functioning at a natural frequency and intensity and were not as influenced, as they are today, by human activities (land clearing, water diversions, etc.).

Native assemblages of fish and wildlife are best restored and maintained by providing a diversity of natural habitats typical of the ecoregion prior to European settlement. Restoring natural diversity is a desired direction for management of the San Joaquin River NWR. Some restoration at the Refuge can be accomplished passively by allowing natural processes to resume. However, because of regional changes in river hydrology, presence of flood control levees, the proliferation of invasive species, as well as other factors, many restoration activities will require direct action, such as planting trees and shrubs, breaching levees, recontouring leveled land, reintroducing wildlife, building water control structures, managing invasive species, rehabilitating derelict building sites, restoring fire regimes, etc. Once restored, various levels of management will be required to replicate natural processes and maintain those habitat conditions in the highly altered San Joaquin Valley ecosystem. This management will range from allowing periodic flood events to inundate and maintain natural river functions in the West Unit floodplain to actively managing wetland units, grazing uplands, mimicking natural fire regimes and controlling invasive weed species.

Objective 1. Restore and enhance 2,500 acres of wetlands, riparian forest and upland habitats on Refuge lands within six years of this plan's approval and restore and enhance an additional 1,000 or more acres by the end of this 15 year planning cycle to provide the diversity of habitats necessary to support native assemblages of fish, wildlife and plants.

Figure 9: Proposed Habitat Management for San Joaquin River NWR

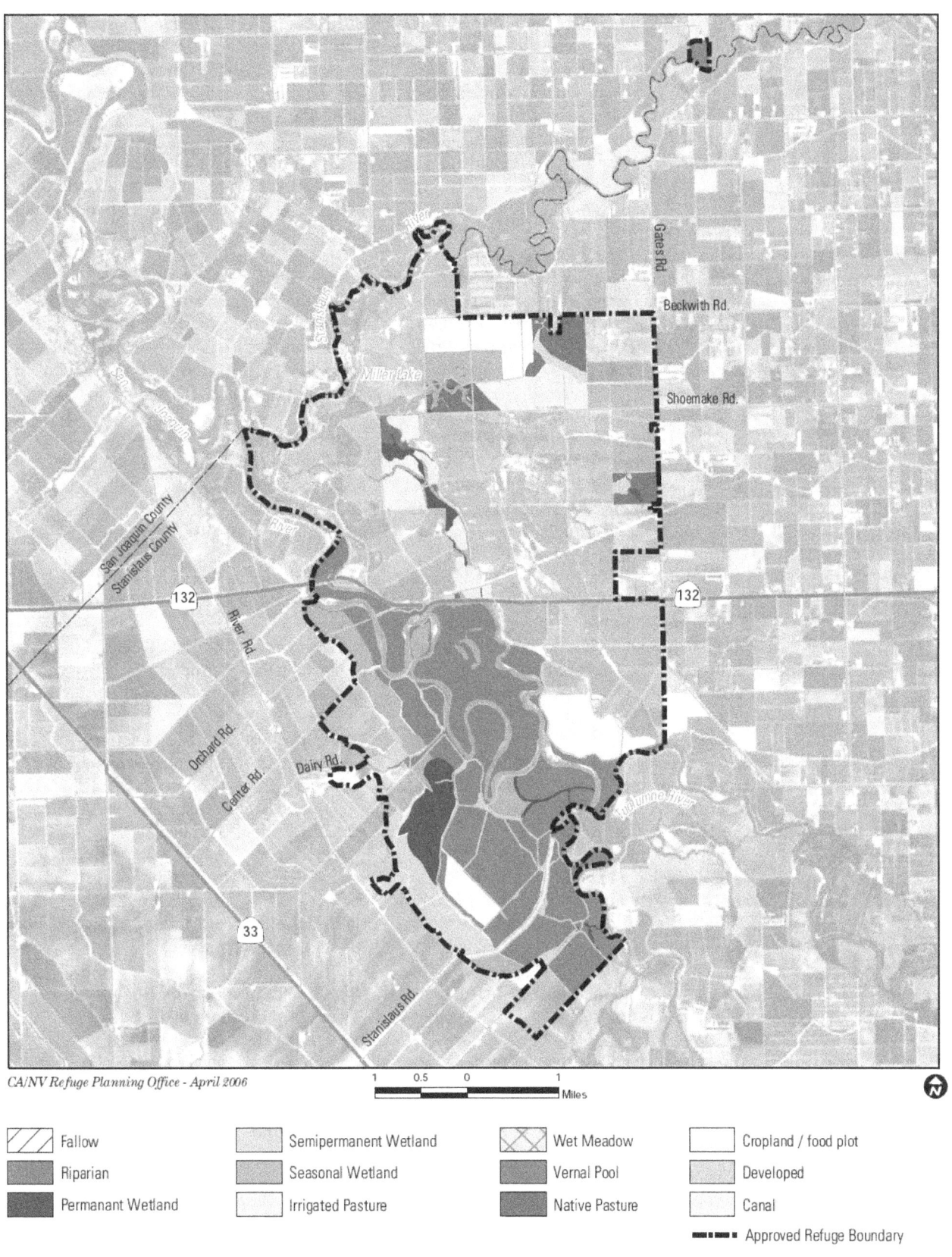

CA/NV Refuge Planning Office - April 2006

Fallow	Semipermanent Wetland	Wet Meadow	Cropland / food plot
Riparian	Seasonal Wetland	Vernal Pool	Developed
Permanant Wetland	Irrigated Pasture	Native Pasture	Canal
			Approved Refuge Boundary

Narrative: Most of the existing Refuge lands have been highly altered through drainage, farming, wildfire suppression and flood control activities. Large scale restoration projects and active management will be required to recreate the natural diversity of habitats found on the floodplain and adjacent uplands of the San Joaquin River.

Strategies:

1.1.1 Complete the wetlands and riparian forest restoration and the uplands enhancement on the West Unit of the San Joaquin River NWR, as identified in the CALFED ERP-01-N08 habitat restoration grant by June 2004.

1.1.2 Coordinate with the staff of the FWS Anadromous Fisheries Recovery Program and other fisheries professionals to ensure that restored wetlands and riparian habitats support and enhance rearing, migration and spawning habitat for native fish species.

1.1.3 Work cooperatively with the U.S. Army Corps of Engineers to breach the flood control levees on Refuge lands west of the San Joaquin River as part of a non-structural flood alternative program and facilitate natural flood events and restore natural floodplain function.

1.1.4 Finalize and implement the restoration plan to create riparian habitat and restore natural floodplain function on the Mohler Tract.

1.1.5 Develop and implement plans to restore and enhance wetland and riparian habitats in the East Unit focusing on the Page/Goose Lake complex, Quesma Field wetlands, Buffington Fields, Riley Slough, Nelson Lake and the Colwell/Christman fields and bottoms.

1.1.6 Develop and implement projects to protect and enhance riparian habitat at Christman Island and the Gardner's Cove area, and restore eroded river stream banks to minimize erosion and subsequent sedimentation.

1.1.7 Develop and implement restoration projects for the remaining fallow agricultural lands outlined in the Pre-Restoration Plan for the West Units of the San Joaquin River NWR, as prepared by River Partners in 2000.

1.1.8 Develop and implement projects to restore the West Unit's current alfalfa field (former Arambel property) to riparian forest.

1.1.9 Prioritize proposed riparian restoration projects with areas and give the highest priority to those that provide corridors from lowland to upland habitats, are within the 100-year floodplain and are adjacent to existing riparian habitat.

1.1.10 Clean up and remove abandoned buildings, farming operation equipment and debris, concrete pads, trash dumps and unneeded fences. Restore these sites to natural habitats.

1.1.11 Prepare a North American Wetlands Conservation Act project proposal for wetlands and riparian habitat restoration/enhancement on the East Unit and parts of the former Vierra property for submittal in 2003 and implement, if funded.

1.1.12 Prepare CALFED habitat restoration proposals (phases 3 and 4 of a 4-phase project) as a follow-up to ERP-01-N08 to continue habitat restoration of the West Unit; implement if funded.

1.1.13 Prepare restoration project funding requests through Service funding programs, the North American Wetlands Conservation Act and other sources.

Objective 2. Manage approximately 700 acres of seasonal wetlands and approximately 750 acres of semipermanent/permanent wetlands to meet the habitat needs of migratory waterfowl, shorebirds, sandhill cranes and other wetland-dependent wildlife.

Narrative: The altered hydrology and loss of historic wetlands in the Central Valley of California requires that natural resource managers actively manage wetland habitats by manipulating water through its delivery and retention and by controlling vegetation and maintaining water control structures in order to provide a diversity of habitats for wetland dependent wildlife species.

Strategies:

1.2.1 Develop a water management facilities inventory and wetland management plan for the San Joaquin River NWR and incorporate both into the San Luis NWR Complex Wetland Management Plan.

1.2.2 Prepare and implement annual draw-down and flood-up plans for seasonal and semipermanent wetlands at the Refuge.

1.2.3 Maintain stable water levels in permanent wetlands such a Miller Lake, Nelson Lake and Lower White Lake to provide summer water and habitat for wildlife and limit encroachment by emergent vegetation.

1.2.4 Maintain a regular schedule of staff gauge water level readings to monitor water management and regulate water control structures and water deliveries to maintain prescribed water levels and provide maintenance flows.

1.2.5 Control excessive robust vegetation (i.e., cockleburr, cattail, roundstem bulrush, etc.) in goose roost ponds and other wetlands through water management practices, pre-flood-up mowing, prescribed burning and herbicide application.

1.2.6 Conduct annual evaluations to see if management objectives are being met, units need to be rehabilitated and water control structures/delivery systems need to be replaced. Schedule and implement unit rehabilitation activities and water control structure/delivery system replacement, as needed.

1.2.7 Record unit prescriptions, management activities, staff gauge readings and other records and incorporate into a long-term database.

Objective 3. Manage 3,500 to 3,700 acres of riparian forest and floodplain habitat to meet the needs of neotropical migratory birds, colonial nesting waterbirds and other riparian forest associated wildlife.

Narrative: Active management of riparian forest and floodplain habitats will be much less intensive than that required for wetlands. Once restored and established, natural processes will dominate in these habitats. Over time, floodwaters coming through the levee breaches will carve out channels and oxbows and recontour the floodplain on the West Unit. In addition, the disturbance effects of periodic flood flows will increase diversity by creating different age and species structures within the riparian forest communities. Nonetheless, certain management practices will be required to offset the impacts of altered hydrology, and to protect riparian habitat from the effects of adjacent land uses and Refuge operations.

Strategies:

1.3.1 Promote the establishment of native riparian trees, shrubs and herbaceous plants after restoration projects are complete through periodic replanting, irrigation and weed control.

1.3.2 Breech levees to allow floodwaters to inundate the West Unit floodplain to benefit riparian habitat systems.

1.3.3 Limit the amount of roads, grazing, food plots and unnecessary disturbance adjacent to riparian habitats to reduce negative edge effects, such as brown-headed cowbird nest parasitism.

1.3.4 Install fences around riparian habitats adjacent to pastures to preclude grazing damage.

1.3.5 Incorporate riparian forest habitat needs into the Refuge fire management plan and annual invasive weed management plans.

1.3.6 Repair eroded stream banks where appropriate to reduce sedimentation and stabilize trees.

Objective 4. Manage 1,250 acres of agricultural lands (irrigated pasture, alfalfa, small cereal grains and corn) and 350 acres of native grasslands and oak savannah uplands to meet the habitat needs of sandhill cranes, arctic-nesting geese, other migratory birds and other grassland associated wildlife.

Narrative: Since the early 1900s many species of migratory birds have become highly dependent on agricultural lands during part of their annual life cycle. There is a long history of geese, sandhill cranes and other migratory birds using the croplands and pastures of the Faith and Mapes Ranches, and that use is a major reason the San Joaquin River NWR was established. In addition, other unique wildlife, such as white-faced ibis and long-billed curlew, heavily use the grasslands and pastures for foraging. A portion of the lands that were farmed or grazed at time of acquisition, especially those on the East Unit, need to remain in that type of management to maintain the resource values that first attracted birds into the area.

Few stands of native grasslands or oak savannah uplands remain in this part of the San Joaquin Valley. It is important that these plant communities on the Refuge be maintained and enhanced for the benefit of ground nesting birds and other wildlife associated with these habitats. Without grazing or other management, these habitats would become infested with invasive weeds, such as yellow starthistle, milk thistle and poison hemlock, thus reducing the habitat quality for wildlife.

Management of the agricultural lands and native grasslands for the benefit of migratory birds and other upland-associated wildlife will be an integral part of the farming and grazing management program (see Goal 3, Objective 6 and Goal 4, Objectives 1 and 2).

Strategies:
1.4.1 Continue livestock grazing through a CLMA on irrigated pasture and native grasslands to maintain short-cropped winter foraging habitat in accordance with annual grazing plans.

1.4.2 Limit grazing on native grasslands from December through May-June to accommodate invasive weed control objectives and allow vegetative growth for ground nesting birds.

1.4.3 Continue growing corn and winter wheat for winter forage through sharecropping agreements and CLMAs.

1.4.4 Begin growing alfalfa by 2004 through a CLMA to provide winter forage for geese and cranes. Work with the CLMA operators on ways to reduce pesticide use and minimize impacts of hay harvest on ground-nesting birds.

1.4.5 Protect existing young valley oak trees in areas being grazed and, where appropriate, plant additional oaks to increase the amount of oak savannah habitat.

1.4.6 Incorporate upland habitat management needs into the Refuge fire management plan and the annual weed management plan.

Objective 5. Within two years, develop and implement an invasive weed management plan to reduce the area coverage of non-native invasive plants that adversely impact native plant and wildlife communities and meet Refuge habitat management objectives.

Narrative: Non-native invasive plants are present at varying degrees throughout the Refuge. They have the potential to dominate sites; in some locations, they have already proliferated, altering the vegetative community, lowering overall diversity and creating marginal or unsuitable habitat conditions for native plants and wildlife. The spread of invasive plants threatens successful restoration of riparian plant communities of the San Joaquin River floodplain, maintenance of current plant communities in existing riparian forest and native grassland habitats, and successful production of wildlife forage in managed wetlands and cropfields. Species of greatest management concern on the Refuge include, but are not limited to, yellow starthistle, perennial pepperweed, arundo, poison hemlock, milk thistle, tobacco tree and salt cedar.

Strategies:

1.5.1 Inventory the occurrence and map the distribution of non-native invasive weeds on the Refuge and incorporate into the GIS database to allow monitoring through time.

1.5.2 Develop and implement an integrated invasive pest management plan for the San Joaquin River NWR. Within the plan include weed management strategies for individual pasture units, cropland fields and native upland units. Incorporate specific needs and constraints associated with invasive management of wetlands, riparian and upland habitats into the plan. Incorporate integrated pest management principles, such as grazing, mowing, burning and herbicide application, into the management plan.

1.5.3 Conduct weed control and monitoring activities on the West Unit as outlined in the CALFED ERP-01-N08 restoration grant.

1.5.4 Use grazing, planting of cover crops and other techniques to control the spread of invasive weeds in the fallow fields of the West Unit until they are planted to native trees and shrubs as part of the ongoing riparian restoration projects.

1.5.5 Assume responsibility for weed control of restored riparian areas in the West Unit after River Partners have met their restoration contract obligations.

1.5.6 Place a high priority on eradicating non-native invasive weed species, such as Russian knapweed and Himalaya berry, that are currently present in low levels but have the potential to become widespread throughout the Refuge.

Prescribed burn by Refuge staff to control invasive plants.
Photo: Perry Grissom

1.5.7 Conduct regular monitoring to assess results of control activities and to detect the presence of any new infestations of current or newly established species.

1.5.8 Continue to participate as a member of the multi-agency Northern San Joaquin Valley Weed Management organization.

1.5.9 Seek opportunities for funding pest management activities through local, State and Federal initiatives.

Objective 6. Within 10 years develop a dependable water supply and delivery system, and ensure that at least 20,000 acre/feet of water is available for Refuge use annually to manage habitats for native assemblages of fish and wildlife.

Narrative: Adequate water supplies and the ability to efficiently move water is a critical component in the management of Refuges in the Central Valley of California. Water will be used on the Refuge to manage wetlands and agricultural habitats and for the restoration of riparian forests.

Strategies:

1.6.1 Document annual water needs, status of existing water delivery infrastructure, existing water rights, water allotment from Modesto Irrigation District, existing well capacity, and potential water sources, and incorporate into a water management plan.

1.6.2 Continue to work with CLMA operators to provide water for management of the Refuge agricultural and wetland habitats.

1.6.3 Use groundwater supplies by upgrading existing wells if feasible and, where necessary, develop new wells to meet the water needs of the Refuge.

1.6.4 Repair and fit with fish screens existing lift pumps on the San Joaquin and Tuolumne rivers so existing riparian rights can be employed for Refuge water needs.

1.6.5 Initiate negotiations with Modesto Irrigation District for additional water supplies to the Refuge. Consider using accretion supplies and well supplies.

1.6.6 Upgrade existing, and where necessary, construct new canals, ditches, pipelines and other water delivery infrastructure facilities necessary to manage existing and proposed Refuge habitats.

Objective 7. Within 10 years ensure that Refuge water supplies meet Regional Water Quality Control Board (RWQCB) standards for use on wetlands and Refuge discharges from managed wetlands do not exceed total daily maximum load limits established by that Board.

Narrative: Water quality is an important aspect of Refuge operations and is critical to maintaining the health and productivity of fish and wildlife communities. Water discharges from the Refuge should not contribute to the degradation of the San Joaquin River. This is complicated by the fact the San Joaquin River, which is the predominant source of water for the West Unit, has been designated as an impaired waterway and the Refuge is forced to accept agricultural surface drainwater from upslope lands.

Strategies:
1.7.1 Collect published reports and documents on the water quality of existing and potential water supplies within five years to determine potential water quality problems.

1.7.2 Develop a monitoring program to determine the baseline water quality for Refuge lands and monitor Refuge water supply quality on a quarterly basis.

1.7.3 Work with local water districts to conduct voluntary assessments of quality of water delivered to the Refuge.

1.7.4 Ensure that water applied to Refuge wetlands does not exceed 2 parts per billion (ppb) selenium (minimum RWQCB standards).

1.7.5 Clean up the dairy waste lagoon at the former Vierra dairy operation to preclude impacts to the Refuge's water quality.

1.7.6 Work with the FWS Sacramento Ecological Services office to fund and implement water quality and contaminants assessments on the Refuge.

1.7.7 Work with NRCS and upstream landowners to reduce sediment loads of drainwaters coming onto the Refuge by implementing recommendations outlined in the U.S. Dept. of Agriculture Sediment Reduction Plan (*USDA 1992*) and, where possible, implement those same recommendations on the Refuge to further reduce sediment flow into the San Joaquin River.

1.7.8 Participate in the Regional Water Quality Control Board process to establish total maximum load limits of salts, boron and other constituents in the San Joaquin River.

Objective 8: Within two years, develop and implement a Refuge inventory and monitoring program that incorporates existing and new surveys/censuses of plants, fish and wildlife, as well as their responses to restoration/management activities that can be employed to guide the management of the Refuge.

Narrative: Knowledge of the distribution and abundance of species, species' needs and status is critical for the management of the Refuge. Biological monitoring is necessary to assess the status of fish and wildlife populations, as well as how they respond to management actions. Management effectiveness can be evaluated and corrected, if needed, based on a monitoring program. Monitoring will consist of both long and short-term projects and be conducted by Complex staff, partners, contractors and other researchers. Some monitoring efforts will be conducted to meet Refuge data needs, while others will contribute to or be a part of larger-scale ecoregion, Flyway or National monitoring initiatives.

Strategies:

1.8.1 Develop and implement a monitoring plan to determine the abundance, distribution and productivity of neotropical migratory landbirds, wetland dependent birds, mammals, reptiles, amphibians and fish using Refuge lands.

1.8.2 Work with both public and private partners to monitor threatened and endangered species found at the Refuge to facilitate their recovery (see Goal 3).

1.8.3 Update inventories of fish, amphibian, reptile, bird and mammal species present in the established and restored waterways, wetlands, riparian areas and uplands of the Refuge.

1.8.4 Develop and implement a habitat monitoring plan to measure habitat changes and results/impacts of restoration efforts.

1.8.5 Expand and update the Refuge GIS database to document habitats, land use practices and restoration project results.

1.8.6 Integrate wildlife population data (i.e., abundance and distribution) with GIS habitat layers to facilitate management actions.

1.8.7 Work with USGS/BRD, universities, organizations and individuals to develop research projects regarding natural resource issues to guide management at the Refuge.

Objective 9. Restore natural processes where possible to ensure ecosystem function.

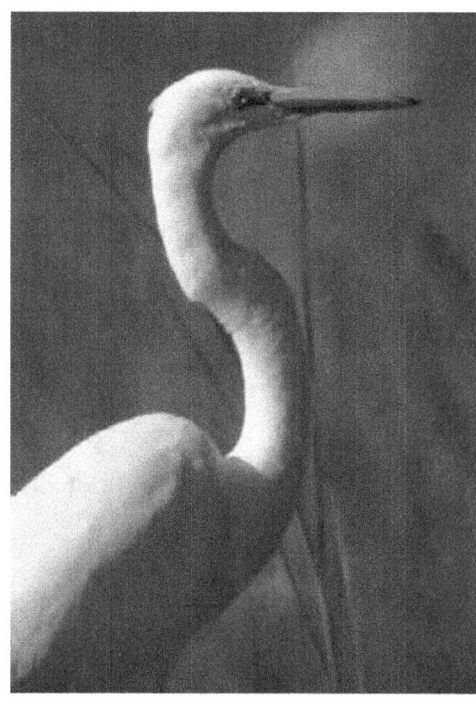

Narrative:

Ecosystem health depends not only on ecosystem components but also, the natural processes that drive ecosystem functions. Many natural processes that are vital to ecosystems, such as river events and wildfire, have been eliminated or suppressed by flood control structures and fire suppression programs respectively. Many of these natural processes maintain ecosystem diversity by their actions. Impediments preventing natural processes to function will be minimized or eliminated, if deemed appropriate.

Great egret, a conspicuous species at the Refuge.
Photo: Jerry Baldwin

Strategies:

1.9.1 Work cooperatively with the U.S. Army Corps of Engineers to breach the flood control levees on Refuge lands west of the San Joaquin River as part of a non-structural flood alternative program and to facilitate natural flood events and restore natural floodplain function. (Same as strategy 1.1.3.)

1.9.2 Finalize and implement the restoration plan to create riparian habitat and restore natural floodplain function on the Mohler Tract. (Same as strategy 1.1.4.)

1.9.3 Develop and implement projects to protect and enhance riparian habitat at Christman Island and the Gardner's Cove area, and restore eroded river stream banks to minimize erosion and subsequent sedimentation. (Same as strategy 1.1.6.)

1.9.4 Ascertain past and suitable fire regimes for habitat types at the San Joaquin River NWR to develop fire plans.

1.9.5 Restore the role of fire through a prescribed fire program at the San Joaquin River NWR.

1.9.6 Work with NRCS and upstream landowners to reduce sediment loads of drainwaters coming onto the Refuge through implementing recommendations outlined in the U.S. Dept. of Agriculture Sediment Reduction Plan (USDA 1992) and, where possible, implement those same recommendations on Refuge to further reduce sediment flow into the San Joaquin River. (Same as strategy 1.7.7.)

Goal 2 (Threatened and Endangered Species)

Contribute to the recovery of threatened/ endangered species, as well as the protection of populations of special status wildlife and plant species and their habitats.

Narrative: Federal and State threatened and endangered species and other special status species are a high priority for the management of the San Joaquin River NWR. The Refuge will aid in the protection and recovery of these species by maintaining and managing the habitats on which they depend, pursuing other measures, as needed, and participating in species recovery efforts.

Objective 1. Reestablish two self-sustaining populations of riparian brush rabbits (Federal/State–Endangered) on Refuge lands within 10 years.

Narrative: The Riparian Brush Rabbit Working Group, comprised of the Service, BOR, CDFG, California Dept. of Parks and Recreation and CSU-Stanislaus Endangered Species Recovery Program is actively working to recover riparian brush rabbits from their endangered species status. With funding from the aforementioned Federal and State agencies, CSU-Stanislaus ESRP has conducted studies to better understand the ecology of the rabbit, established and run a captive propagation facility, released rabbits on the Refuge in 2002/03 to establish

a population and is monitoring the status of the released rabbits.

The Refuge is within the historic range of the riparian brush rabbit and is in proximity to an existing population at Caswell State Park. It has high potential to support the long term establishment of brush rabbit populations. The necessary habitat features required to enhance the area for this species include increasing the amount of California blackberry, California rose and other dense growing shrubs/forbs; expanding the riparian forest on the San Joaquin River floodplain; and creating vegetated, elevated mounds to provide refugia for the rabbits during flood events.

Strategies:
2.1.1 Continue to work with ESRP and participate as a member of the Riparian Brush Rabbit Recovery Working Group to introduce captive-bred brush rabbits at two separate release sites and assist in monitoring their survival, productivity and distribution.

2.1.2 Create elevated, earthen mounds in the floodplain to provide refugia during flood events and vegetate these areas with native blackberry, rose and herbaceous plants as escape cover.

2.1.3 Establish thick stands of native blackberry and rose along the banks of levees and ensure that patches of these plants are incorporated in riparian forest restoration plantings within the floodplain.

2.1.4 Increase the amount of riparian forest habitat and ensure that a mix of riparian forest growth stages exist on the Refuge.

Objective 2. Maintain and enhance at least one self-sustaining population of San Joaquin Valley woodrats (Federal—Endangered) on Refuge lands consistent with recovery actions and other parameters established by the FWS Endangered Species Office.

Narrative: San Joaquin Valley woodrat recovery efforts are being conducted in coordination with many of the participants of the riparian brush rabbit recovery program. CSU-Stanislaus ESRP is conducting research and monitoring at nearby Caswell State Park to better understand the ecology of the woodrat and the impacts of competition by non-native black rats. However, no direct management recovery actions are occurring for the species. The Refuge is within the historic range of the San Joaquin Valley woodrat, but it is unknown to what extent they presently occur at the Refuge.

Strategies:
2.2.1 Determine the level of occurrence of the San Joaquin Valley woodrat at the San Joaquin River NWR.

2.2.2 Work with the FWS Endangered Species Office, ESRP and other partners to evaluate the suitability of habitat and feasibility, if needed, of reestablishing/maintaining woodrats on the Refuge.

2.2.3 Participate in and foster any on-Refuge population management projects initiated by the FWS Endangered Species Office.

Objective 3. Protect populations of vernal pool fairy shrimp (multiple species Federal–Endangered), vernal pool tadpole shrimp (Federal–Endangered) and California tiger salamander (Federal–Candidate) by maintaining existing vernal pools (15 total; combined size < 1.0 ac.), associated plant communities and surrounding micro-watersheds.

Narrative: Multiple species of fairy shrimp, as well as vernal pool tadpole shrimp and California tiger salamanders, depend on vernal pools for survival. The most important components of preserving vernal pools are maintaining their natural hydrology. Vernal pools are supplied entirely by rainwater. To protect vernal pool habitats, the integrity of the underlaying claypan of the basin and topography of the micro-watershed must be preserved. An additional problem for vernal pools is that during dry years, upland plant species tend to encroach in the dry vernal pools, which

results in thatch accumulation that hinders the growth of vernal pool plant species.

Strategies:
2.3.1 Map locations of vernal pools on the Refuge GIS database and document status of individual vernal pool communities.

2.3.2 Continue the Complex-wide policy of no alteration of the topography of native uplands.

2.3.3 Use grazing to maintain short grass plant communities (3–6 in. high) and reduce thatch accumulation around vernal pool habitats.

Objective 4. Complete an abundance and distribution inventory of valley elderberry longhorn beetle (Federal–Endangered), giant garter snake (Federal–Threatened), willow flycatcher (State–Endangered) and western yellow-billed cuckoo (State–Endangered) on the San Joaquin River NWR. Develop Refuge management plans for the species, if deemed necessary, within 10 years.

Narrative: Little is known regarding the status of these species on the Refuge. Information is required to determine if Refuge habitats are suitable for supporting populations of these species, and if they currently exist on the Refuge. Once their distribution and abundance on the Refuge is determined, restoration and management of habitats to meet species needs can be implemented, if needed and direct participation in recovery efforts initiated, as appropriate.

Strategies:
2.4.1 Seek funding for species and habitat inventories through CALFED grants, FWS/RONS projects, or other funding sources, and conduct inventories when funded.

2.4.2 Ascertain the distribution and abundance of valley elderberry longhorn beetle, giant garter snake, willow flycatcher and western yellow-billed cuckoo on the Refuge.

2.4.3 Incorporate the species and habitat inventories into the Refuge GIS database.

2.4.4 Develop and implement species management plans that incorporate habitat requirements from the literature and guidelines from species recovery plans.

Objective 5. Provide and enhance migration, spawning and rearing habitat for fall-run Chinook salmon Federal–Threatened), Central Valley steelhead (Federal–Threatened), Sacramento splittail (Federal–Threatened), and any other listed fish species by establishing and maintaining a minimum of seven miles of shaded riverine aquatic habitat and 3,500 acres of floodplain habitat along the San Joaquin, Stanislaus and Tuolumne Rivers.

Narrative: The Refuge is downstream from tributaries where Chinook salmon and steelhead spawn and within the spawning area for Sacramento splittail. These species are currently excluded from most of the Refuge floodplain by the presence of flood control levees. Breaching on-Refuge levees as part of floodplain restoration and as an alternative flood control project will allow the river to assume a more natural pattern of flooding and inundation, giving these and other special status native fish species access to the floodplain during flood events. During periods of inundation, the restored floodplain can provide valuable spawning and rearing habitat for Sacramento splittail, and rearing habitat for salmon and steelhead smolts, thus contributing to the recovery these listed species. However, if designed or managed incorrectly, floodplain channels and wetlands could cause stranding and mortality of these same fish as the floodwater recedes. In addition, operation of any unscreened Refuge lift pumps along the San Joaquin, Tuolumne, and Stanislaus rivers could result in fish mortality.

Strategies:
2.5.1 Coordinate with staff from the FWS-Anadromous Fish Restoration Program and National Marine Fisheries Service to ensure that levee breaching and floodplain restoration is designed and implemented in ways that maximize spawning and rearing habitat benefits to listed and special status fish species, while minimizing potential for stranding.

2.5.2 Implement levee breaching and riparian floodplain restoration as outlined in the CALFED ERP-01-N08 habitat restoration grant.

2.5.3 Develop a fisheries management strategy that is compatible with other Refuge management objectives and maximizes habitat benefits to listed and special status fish species.

2.5.4 Work with partners to evaluate floodplain rearing potential, conduct monitoring to document actual use by and benefits to listed and special status species, and resolve any fisheries issues on Refuge lands.

2.5.5 Install fish screens on all Refuge riverine lift pumps to avoid entrapment of juvenile Chinook salmon, steelhead, Sacramento splittail or any other special status species of fish.

2.5.6 Seek funding sources and establish partnerships to continue additional riparian floodplain restoration and implement projects when funded.

Objective 6. Provide winter foraging and roost habitat for greater sandhill cranes (State–Threatened) by managing and enhancing 830 acres of irrigated pastures and native grasslands, 550 acres of corn and cereal grain fields and 400 acres of roost pond habitat in conjunction with Aleutian Canada goose and other migratory bird management.

Narrative: Greater sandhill cranes winter on the Refuge in association with larger numbers of lesser sandhill cranes. Cranes are highly dependent on croplands and irrigated pasture, as well as native grasslands, for foraging habitat. They require shallow, open wetlands for use as mid-day loafing sites and night roosts.

Cranes are less tolerant of disturbance than most other migratory birds using the Refuge. Management actions for greater sandhill cranes will be an integral part of the overall management of wetlands and uplands for migratory birds and other wildlife (See Goal 1, Objectives 2 and 4, and for Aleutian Canada geese see Goal 4.)

Strategies:
2.6.1 Continue livestock grazing or other suitable methods on irrigated pasture and native grasslands to maintain short-cropped winter foraging habitat in accordance with annual grazing plans through a CLMA.

2.6.2 Continue growing corn and winter wheat for winter forage through sharecropping agreements and CLMAs.

2.6.3 Where compatible with other foraging habitat objectives, allow winter wheat to mature over the summer and then mow or disc down standing wheat to provide forage for cranes during autumn and early winter.

2.6.4 Manage wetlands to provide shallow (< 1 ft. deep) open loafing areas and roost sites.

2.6.5 Limit disturbance in crane roosts and foraging areas by maintaining sanctuaries.

2.6.6 Participate with other agencies and researchers in conducting Flyway-wide population surveys, population monitoring and other research.

Objective 7: Provide habitat for and monitor least Bell's vireo at the Refuge.

Narrative: This endangered species was first detected nesting on the refuge in 2005. The vireo nested in recently restored riparian habitat. It is likely that the riparian habitat being restored at the Refuge will provide additional habitat for this endangered species as well as other riparian dependent wildlife.

Strategies:
2.7.1 Monitor presence and abundance of breeding pairs of least Bell's vireo at the Refuge.

2.7.2 Document vegetation characteristics of vireo nesting habitat and use to guide riparian restoration and riparian woodland management.

2.7.3 Manage and restore 3,500 acres of riparian habitat at the Refuge.

Goal 3 (Aleutian Canada Goose)

Provide optimum wintering habitat for Aleutian Canada geese to ensure the continued recovery from threatened and endangered species status.

Narrative: Although Aleutian Canada geese have been delisted from threatened species status, they remain a species (subspecies) of special emphasis. Mandates of the Endangered Species Act and Service policies direct that management actions be taken to ensure that recovery is maintained. Because the Refuge continues to be the most important wintering area for Aleutian Canada geese and is critical for continued recovery, management to provide winter habitat will remain a priority of the Refuge.

Objective 1. Manage and enhance a minimum of 500 acres of irrigated pasture and 350 acres of native grasslands as short grass foraging habitat (< 8 inches high) through grazing and other pasture management activities for Aleutian Canada geese and other wildlife.

Narrative: Availability of short-cropped tender grasses is a critical component of the winter forage base for this small race of Canada goose. The birds feed on the fast-growing meristems (tips of the plants), which are the most tender portion of the plant and where the highest protein levels are concentrated. Aleutian Canada geese heavily use irrigated pasture during initial arrival in October and November, and irrigated pasture and native grasslands during late January until their departure in April. The availability of this habitat is especially important during the early spring months as the geese switch from a maintenance diet dominated by corn (high carbohydrate) to a higher protein grass diet to build fat reserves to meet the physiological needs associated with migration and subsequent reproduction.

Grazing is the current, preferred method of maintaining short grass conditions rather than mowing, because grazing has proved to be compatible with goose use, is more economical than mowing and does not promote thatch build-up. Grazing is conducted at the Refuge by private individuals through a CLMA.

Strategies:

3.1.1 Continue grazing on irrigated pasture and native grasslands via a CLMA(s) as needed in accordance with annual grazing plans.

3.1.2 Use a combination of force account and CLMA operators to mow and apply herbicides to irrigated pasture, as necessary, to control weeds such as cockleburr, milk thistle and yellow starthistle.

3.1.3 Work with CLMA operators to temporarily flood portions of pastures that receive high goose and other wildlife use during October and November to create wet meadow conditions.

3.1.4 Submit a FWS/RONS proposal to rehabilitate a rank pasture in the Johnson Corral Field and implement, if funded.

Objective 2. Provide a minimum of 115 acres of grain corn and 430 acres of winter wheat and maintain an additional 200 acres of foraging habitat by 2004.

Narrative: Most species of geese in North America, including Aleutian Canada geese, have become dependent on agricultural crops for their winter forage base. Growing grain (corn) and green forage (winter wheat and alfalfa) on the Refuge provides a high quality diet to meet the nutritional needs of wintering Aleutian Canada geese and reduces the amount of crop depredation caused by geese on nearby private lands. The carbohydrates provided by corn are important in maintaining body condition during the winter months and corn forms the major part of the diet from late November to early February. Winter wheat and alfalfa are heavily used by the geese from the time of initial arrival in October until final departure in April. As with grass, the higher protein levels associated with winter wheat and alfalfa are important in building fat reserves for spring migration and the subsequent reproductive cycle.

Geese using crop field on Refuge.
Photo: Gary Powell

However, by late February, much of the winter wheat has been eaten out, or where not foraged upon, has grown too tall and rank to be attractive to geese.

Strategies:

3.2.1 Continue growing corn and winter wheat on the East Unit through use of share cropping agreements and CLMAs.

3.2.2 Reduce reliance on share cropping of corn if the CLMA program is expanded (on any newly acquired lands or alfalfa fields) and sufficient CLMA credits are generated to allow direct funding of corn production.

3.2.3 Grow approximately 80 acres of winter wheat through a CLMA or force account on the West Unit.

3.2.4 Mow standing corn in sequential blocks from late November to early January to provide grain forage.

3.2.5 Assume management of alfalfa fields in the North/South Christman Fields after December 2003 through a CLMA.

3.2.6 Maintain an additional 200 acres of goose foraging habitat by CLMA in the agricultural field north of Beckwith Road (Buffington property) if the parcel is acquired.

Objective 3. Manage Page, Goose and Nelson Lakes (250 acres combined) as roosting and loafing habitat, and create a 60-acre roost pond in the Christman/ Colwell Fields area by 2010.

Narrative: Shallow wetlands that provide areas for mid-day loafing and night roosts are a critical component of wintering habitat for Aleutian Canada geese. These areas are necessary for resting, preening, maintaining social bonds and providing security from predators. Important features of such roost ponds include an open aspect with limited emergent cover that has islands with low vegetative cover and having an open shoreline on at least part of the wetland. Page, Goose and Nelson Lakes have been the main roost pond sites to date,

but additional roosting and loafing habitat will be necessary as the goose population increases.

Strategies:

3.3.1 Maintain Page and Goose Lakes as open aspect seasonal wetlands and Nelson Lake as a permanent pond.

3.3.2 Graze or mow shorelines and islands of roost ponds prior to flood-up to provide loafing habitat for geese.

3.3.3 Create and subsequently manage as a seasonal wetland a 60-acre roost pond on the west side of the Christman/Colwell Field area adjacent to the San Joaquin River levee.

Objective 4. Provide 1,200 -1,400 acres of sanctuary in the foraging and roost areas of the East Unit by minimizing disturbance from public use and other disturbance factors in those areas.

Narrative: Migratory birds, including Aleutian Canada geese, require disturbance-free areas in which to rest and feed. Although Aleutian Canada geese can be tolerant of human presence in certain feeding areas at the Refuge, excessive disturbance causes birds to flush and relocate to other areas, resulting in loss of feeding opportunity, expenditure of nutrient reserves and added stress. These impacts are especially critical in late winter and early spring, when geese are actively acquiring nutrient reserves for spring migration and the subsequent reproductive cycle.

Strategies:

3.4.1 Restrict public use in the Goose Lake/ Page Lake and Dairy Field/Page Field area to the viewing platform site along Beckwith Road.

3.4.2 Design any photo blind or walking trail developed east of the Dairy Field so that disturbance to Aleutian Canada geese and other migratory birds is minimized.

3.4.3 Keep Johnson Corral fields, Beet Field, Maze Bottoms, 90-Acre Field and

Colwell/Christman fields and bottoms closed to public use.

Objective 5. Minimize losses to avian cholera and other diseases by conducting regular disease monitoring annually from December through April and by management of roost pond water levels.

Narrative: Avian cholera is the primary disease that affects waterbirds at the Refuge and in the Northern San Joaquin Valley. Recent research indicates that the bacterium is endemic in certain waterfowl populations and that outbreaks can be triggered by bird to bird transmission during periods of overcrowding and stress. Birds can die quickly after exposure and once an outbreak occurs, large numbers can die in a short period of time. Past outbreaks at the Refuge have coincided with the presence of large numbers of snow and Ross' geese and periods of cold foggy weather.

Strategies:
3.5.1 Conduct weekly surveys for the presence of sick or dead geese around the roost ponds from December through April. Survey frequency will be increased during periods of cold, foggy weather or if diseased birds are encountered.

3.5.2 Monitor turbidity of water in roost ponds and provide flushing flows to maintain good water quality and clarity.

3.5.3 Implement disease outbreak notification and control activities procedures as outlined in   the
San Luis NWR Complex Disease Contingency Plan and the Aleutian Canada Goose Disease and Contamination Hazard Contingency Plan. In the annual work plan, a Refuge staff member will be given responsibility for disease monitoring, notification and coordination of disease control activities

3.5.4 Submit specimens picked up in disease control activities to the National Wildlife Health Research Center for official confirmation of disease outbreaks.

3.5.5 Incorporate documentation of disease losses and disease control activities into the San Luis NWR Complex-wide annual disease reports.

Objective 6. Manage habitat and populations in the context of FWS post-delisting obligations and Pacific Flyway management objectives.

Narrative: The Endangered Species Act requires that species be monitored for five years following delisting to ensure recovery goals remain accomplished. Once Aleutian Canada geese were delisted, management authority shifted from the Service's Endangered Species Office to its Migratory Bird Management Office, and the species was incorporated into the Flyway Council process. An Aleutian Canada Goose Management Plan, which will be updated every five years, has been approved by the Pacific Flyway Council. Since most of the Aleutian Canada goose population winters on the Refuge, management and monitoring actions taken here will be coordinated with, and be an integral part of, larger scale population management of the subspecies.

Strategies:
3.6.1 Coordinate with the FWS Region 7 Endangered Species Office on recovery issues for the five years following delisting.

3.6.2 Participate as an advisor of the Aleutian Canada Goose Management Subcommittee of the Pacific Flyway Study Group.

3.6.3 Monitor Aleutian Canada goose use of the Refuge and surrounding lands to determine numbers present, evaluate effectiveness of habitat management and document crop depredation issues.

3.6.4 Band and neck-collar geese on an annual basis in partnership with California Department of Fish and Game.

3.6.5 Conduct population and off-Refuge distribution monitoring to the extent permitted by funding from the Endangered Species or Migratory Bird programs.

GOAL 4 (Ecosystem Management)

Coordinate the natural resource management of the San Joaquin River National Wildlife Refuge within the context of the larger Central Valley/San Francisco Ecoregion.

Narrative: Although the San Joaquin River NWR contains significant wildlife resources, including on a national level for species such as the Aleutian Canada goose and riparian brush rabbit, the surrounding land use and its management impacts the natural resources within the Refuge. Working cooperatively with both public and private entities provides the opportunity to affect natural resource management on a landscape or ecoregion level. Resources of the Refuge which can be addressed at this larger scale include migratory birds, anadromous fish, water issues, endangered and threatened species, contaminants, habitat patch size and riparian corridors, amongst others.

The U.S. Fish and Wildlife Service has divided the nation into ecoregions to coordinate natural resource management. The San Joaquin River NWR is situated in the Central Valley/San Francisco ecoregion which includes the San Joaquin and Sacramento valleys and their drainages, as well as the Sacramento delta. This ecoregion contains significant wetland habitats which support some of the largest waterfowl and waterbird concentrations in the Pacific Flyway.

Objective 1. Seek the acquisition of lands for the San Joaquin River NWR from within the approved Refuge boundary from willing landowners.

Narrative: Approximately half the acreage in the approved Refuge boundary has been purchased. The remaining lands are in private ownership. These lands have been previously identified as having suitable or potential significant wildlife values. Acquisition of lands within the approved Refuge boundary will enhance existing wildlife resources on present Refuge lands and enhance wildlife resources by increasing the land base; it will also provide for increased flexibility in the management of wildlife resources and offer greater opportunities for wildlife-dependent public use at the Refuge.

Strategies:
4.1.1 Maintain a database of private lands within the approved Refuge boundary.

4.1.2 Work with the Service's Region 1 Realty Office on the acquisition of the Buffington parcel.

4.1.3 Work with the Service's Region 1 Realty Office on the acquisition of any private land parcels within the approved Refuge boundary as they become available from willing sellers.

Objective 2. Identify and acquire lands, outside the current acquisition boundary, with key natural resource features appropriate for inclusion into the San Joaquin River National Wildlife Refuge.

Narrative: Opportunities to benefit wildlife at the San Joaquin River NWR exist outside of the present Refuge acquisition boundary. Lands outside the current boundary offer the potential for increasing the amount of both wetland and riparian habitats, as well as offering the possibilities for increasing the connectivity of Refuge lands with similar wildlands in the San Joaquin Valley.

Strategies:
4.2.1 Expand the San Luis NWR Complex's Geographic Information System (GIS) capabilities over the next ten years to include lands outside the acquisition

White-crowned sparrow, a common winter songbird.

boundary of the San Joaquin River NWR, particularly in regards to riparian corridors.

4.2.2 Identify lands outside of the approved acquisition boundary for the San Joaquin River NWR which have key or the potential for key natural resources and/or would protect or enhance existing Refuge resources.

4.2.3 Work with the Service's Region 1 Realty Office to expand the Refuge's acquisition boundary, if deemed appropriate, for the acquisition of land currently outside the boundary.

Objective 3. Manage the U.S. Fish and Wildlife Service's easement program on private lands for the benefit of wildlife within the acquisition boundary of the San Joaquin River NWR and explore the potential for additional wildlife easements in the vicinity of the Refuge.

Narrative: Service easements on private lands provide benefits to wildlife at lower cost than Refuge land acquisition, although they do not provide the same degree of flexibility of land management and overall benefit to wildlife. However, easements provide an opportunity to increase the level of protected habitats for wildlife surrounding Refuge lands and yield added benefits for wildlife when full land acquisition is neither feasible nor desirable.

*Strategies***:**
4.3.1 Monitor existing easement agreements with private landowners to ensure program compliance and wildlife benefits.

4.3.2 Identify and implement natural resource projects to benefit wildlife on easement lands to be funded through the Service's Partners for Fish and Wildlife Program or other funding mechanisms.

4.3.3 Seek additional lands within the Refuge's acquisition boundary for the Service easement program, if deemed appropriate.

Objective 4. Create and cultivate partnerships, wherever possible, with other landowners including agencies, organizations, businesses, universities and/or private individuals, to coordinate and foster natural resource management in the ecoregion.

Narrative: In addition to Refuge management, other ecosystem management efforts are being undertaken along this portion of the San Joaquin River. The U.S. Army Corps of Engineers' Comprehensive Study (see Chapter 1, Other Projects), the San Joaquin River Management Plan, NRCS' Wetlands Reserve Program and others are seeking to connect natural lands and foster natural resource management along the San Joaquin River. Refuge involvement with these initiatives will provide greater benefits for wildlife and the San Joaquin River NWR.

*Strategies***:**
4.4.1 Provide natural resource information collected at the San Joaquin River NWR to other interested agencies, groups and researchers to foster collaborative efforts and support ecoregion-wide natural resource databases.

4.4.2 Participate in the regional planning for the conservation of the riparian brush rabbit, San Joaquin Valley woodrat, Aleutian Canada goose, California tiger salamander, vernal pool communities, San Joaquin kit fox and other species of special concern.

4.4.3 Participate in joint natural resource projects at the ecoregion level involving partners on issues pertaining to the management and protection of resources at the San Joaquin River NWR.

4.4.4 Develop a Refuge Friends group with interested parties for either the San Joaquin River NWR or the San Luis NWR Complex to promote and foster the natural resources of the Refuge and ecoregion. (Same as strategy 5.9.5.)

Objective 5. Foster natural resource research opportunities on the San Joaquin River National Wildlife Refuge for investigators involved in ecoregion-wide research efforts.

Narrative: Natural resource management direction and techniques employed at National Wildlife Refuges are developed through cooperative and coordinated research projects between the Refuge and investigators. All major advances and improvements in natural resource management at Refuges are developed through the research process.

Strategies:
4.5.1 Encourage universities and researchers conducting ecoregion natural resource investigations to include the San Joaquin River NWR.

Goal 5 (Public Use of the Refuge)

Provide the public with opportunities for compatible, wildlife-dependent visitor services to enhance understanding, appreciation and enjoyment of natural resources at the San Joaquin River NWR.

Narrative: Wildlife-dependent recreational activities, as identified in the Refuge Improvement Act, were given primary consideration over all other public uses. These wildlife-dependent priority public uses were considered and analyzed for implementation at the Refuge. These six priority uses include hunting, fishing, wildlife observation, wildlife photography, environmental education and interpretation. Existing public uses for the Refuge are limited to wildlife viewing and photography from an observation platform, occasional interpretive walks or programs, and guided visits for schoolchildren.

Planning for visitor services is influenced by other criteria, including wildlife needs, land use, habitat and wildlife protection, as well as accommodating the public's desire for different types of recreational activities and the potential for one activity to impact others. The Refuge's relatively small size and site specific issues that guided the development of habitat management required a similarly habitat-driven development for visitor services.

Objective 1: Implement a wildlife observation and photography program for the public on the San Joaquin River NWR by developing five public use facilities within the next five years and within the following five years, develop an additional five public use facilities.

Narrative: The Refuge's proximity to and access from major California highways and population centers provides numerous and constant opportunities for the general public and groups to visit, enjoy and learn about the Refuge and its wildlife resources. Two major highways flank the Refuge, providing convenient access for the public. Major population centers in proximity to the Refuge include Modesto, Stockton, Sacramento and San Francisco.

The general area is lacking in other public-owned wildlands, where the public has the opportunity to enjoy and view wildlife, plants and habitats. A public use program at the Refuge will help to fill a regional need for outdoor recreation with a focus on wildlife.

Strategies:
5.1.1 Prepare and begin implementation of a public use plan focusing on wildlife observation, photography, environmental education and nature interpretation at the San Joaquin River NWR. The plan will integrate all aspects of a public use program with the other programs at the Refuge. This plan will be completed within three years and provide specific guidance for program implementation.

5.1.2 Construct either an auto-tour route or foot-trail that features wildlife observation and photographic opportunities for the public through a diverse array of habitats on the west side of the San Joaquin River. The tour route or foot-trail will include route/trail surface modification, signage, information kiosk, observation platform(s), side foot-trails, brochures and maps, among other features.

5.1.3 Complete the wildlife observation platform and kiosk on Beckwith Road (landscaping, interpretive panels, parking lot improvements and signage).

5.1.4 Develop and construct two wildlife-photography blinds at the Refuge.

5.1.5 Develop part of Christman Island as a free-roaming birding and wildlife viewing area. Construct a trail from a developed parking area to the wildlife viewing area and develop signage and maps to restrict public access from sensitive natural resource areas on Christman Island.

5.1.6 Develop one or more walk-in car-top boat launching facilities to facilitate the public's ability to view wildlife from small watercraft and to promote recreational angling.

5.1.7 Develop the Gardener's Cove area as a visitor use area (i.e., wildlife observation and photography as well as recreational angling), if deemed safe and compatible with the proposed Caltrans expansion of Highway 132. The current roadway is not safe; before this area can be opened to the public, the Refuge must complete coordination with Caltrans designers and engineers to create a safe entrance and exit.

5.1.8 Develop maps and guides showing visitor facilities and wildlife viewing areas at the Refuge. Develop interpretive materials to promote public use and understanding of the Refuge and the role it plays in the Central Valley Ecosystem and Pacific Flyway.

Objective 2. Within 10 years, develop a visitor contact station and trailhead in proximity to and in coordination with development of the Refuge's headquarters area on Dairy Road.

Narrative: A visitor contact station will be a center for visitor orientation and information at the Refuge. The contact station will provide visitors their first impression of the Refuge and parking, access to an auto tour route and/or nature trails, and a locale to begin their wildlife observation hikes, garner information about opportunities on the Refuge, and learn about the Refuge from interpretive displays and materials.

The main administrative headquarters for the Refuge are in the buildings of a former dairy. This existing complex is close to the center of the Refuge and provides easy access and security for visitor services activities and opportunities to coordinate visitor services with Refuge maintenance and management programs. Visitor access to many parts of the Refuge will be possible after restoration and maintenance programs have been developed for the West Unit.

Strategies:
5.2.1 Construct and install an informational and interpretive kiosk at Dairy Road, serving as the main visitor contact station on the Refuge. Provide an associated 20 vehicle parking lot (with the capacity for two school buses).

5.2.2 Develop and install entrance, directional and regulatory signs at public access areas.

5.2.3 Construct restroom facilities adjacent to the visitor contact station.

5.2.4 Ensure the main auto-tour route or foot-trail (strategy 5.1.2) is in proximity to and accessible via the main visitor contact station.

Objective 3. Within five years, develop and implement a recreational hunt program.

Narrative: Recreational hunting is one of the six priority public uses for the National Wildlife Refuge System. Recreational waterfowl hunting has a long tradition in California's Central Valley. A step-down management plan will be prepared prior to implementing hunting of migratory and upland birds after population monitoring indicates a hunting program could be sustained. This plan would identify suitable hunting areas and game species on the Refuge and the means to implement a hunt program on those areas. If conditions warrant, opportunities to hunt waterfowl would be available in select wetland areas and opportunities to hunt dove, quail and/or other species would be available in upland areas. Hunting opportunities may be limited by time of day, season, game species, numbers of permits issued and may also include a youth and/or disabilities component. Special consideration will be taken to ensure that the recently delisted Aleutian Canada goose population is not adversely affected by hunting on the Refuge.

Strategies:

5.3.1 Evaluate the potential for a recreational hunt program at the San Joaquin River NWR and if warranted develop and implement the step-down hunt management plan.

5.3.2 Coordinate with the California Department of Fish and Game (CDFG) in the development and administration of a recreational hunt program on the Refuge.

5.3.3 Develop maps showing facilities and hunt areas and distribute Refuge program pamphlets to participating sportsmen during the process of implementing a recreational hunting program.

5.3.4 Develop seasonal parking areas, travel routes and provide comfort stations for the hunt program.

5.3.5 Provide sanctuaries for the Aleutian Canada geese and ensure the protection of all threatened and endangered species, as well as other resources.

Objective 4. Develop and implement a recreational fishing program at the San Joaquin River NWR within 10 years.

Narrative: The presence of three rivers on the San Joaquin River NWR offers a variety of fishing opportunities. Gardner's Cove provides one good possibility for bank fishing. Safe access will be available to the site once the Caltrans extension of Highway

132 is completed. Boat and bank fishing opportunities are also possible in the West Unit along the San Joaquin River.

Strategies:

5.4.1 Work and coordinate with CDFG and the FWS Stockton Fishery Office to develop a recreational fishing program on the Refuge. Develop and implement a recreational fishing and boating section in the step-down Public Use Plan for the San Joaquin River NWR (See strategy 5.1.1.)

5.4.2 Develop one or more walk-in car-top boat launching facilities (as per strategy 5.1.6) to promote and facilitate recreational angling.

5.4.3 Provide opportunities for both recreational angling from a boat and the shore after finding suitable locations for these activities that minimize shoreline damage and potential conflicts with sensitive natural resources, as well as other public use programs at the Refuge.

5.4.4 Develop access for recreational fishermen and other visitors at the Gardner's Cove portion of the San Joaquin River NWR once the Caltrans expansion of Highway 132 is completed.

5.4.5 Create and distribute a fact sheet on the Refuge fishing program to the public.

Objective 5. Within five years, establish four interpretive programs, facilities, or publications for a diverse audience that reveals the natural and cultural history of the Refuge, migratory birds, endangered species, natural habitats, habitat restoration programs, wetland ecosystems amongst other topics. Establish an additional four programs, facilities, or publications during the following five years.

Narrative: Organized, well-managed, effective interpretive programs greatly enhance the quality of the public's wildlife experience during their visits and field trips to National Wildlife Refuges.

Strategies:

5.5.1 Develop interpretive programs and events that incorporate Refuge themes and reveal the natural and cultural history of the area.

5.5.2 Construct interpretive kiosks at the observation platform on Beckwith Road and the headquarters' visitor contact station.

5.5.3 Develop and provide maps, brochures and other interpretive materials showing visitor facilities. Distribute Refuge pamphlets at entrance stations to help visitors orient and appreciate the Refuge and the role it plays in the Central Valley ecosystem and the Pacific Flyway.

Objective 6. Develop and implement an environmental education program at the San Joaquin River NWR. Facilitate the use of the Refuge by educational groups.

Narrative: Environmental education serves many purposes including showcasing the Refuge's unique resources in a controlled setting and fostering public education of the Refuge, wildlife and natural resources. Students provided environmental educational opportunities frequently understand the uniqueness of the Refuge and its fish and wildlife and develop a greater appreciation and sense of ownership for the Refuge. School

groups and other educational groups from San Joaquin, Stanislaus and Merced counties will be encouraged to use the Refuge.

Strategies:

5.6.1 Develop an educator-led age-appropriate curriculum for school children that is specific to the resources and goals of the San Joaquin River NWR.

5.6.2 Develop outdoor educational facilities, restroom facilities, parking, guides and other infrastructure necessary to accommodate school groups and buses.

5.6.3 Create an outreach program to recruit and educate teachers to use the Refuge for their environmental education programs.

5.6.4 Expand school use of the San Joaquin River NWR within five years to include four college or university groups and four secondary/primary school groups per annum.

5.6.5 Promote partnerships with educational groups (i.e., such as the existing partnership with the Modesto Rotary Club) to foster and facilitate environmental education opportunities at the San Joaquin River NWR.

Objective 7. Ensure public safety and security at the San Joaquin River NWR.

Narrative: A law enforcement presence at National Wildlife Refuges is crucial for the protection of the public and natural resources. Refuge law enforcement programs are proactive and seek to inform the public regarding Refuge regulations and prevent problems, rather than only enforcing statutes.

Strategies:

5.7.1 Use signs, brochures/fact sheets and the Complex's website to provide Refuge regulations to the visiting public.

5.7.2 Conduct periodic patrols by Refuge law enforcement staff at the San Joaquin River NWR to ensure compliance with Refuge regulations, public safety and natural resource protection.

Environmental education at the Refuge.
Photo: USFWS

5.7.3 Routinely examine and maintain public use facilities at the San Joaquin River NWR to determine and remedy unsafe conditions.

5.7.4 Extinguish all wildfires immediately on the San Joaquin River NWR by following the San Luis NWR Complex dispatch plan. Evacuate the public from the Refuge in the event of wildfire in public use areas.

Objective 8. Develop a public outreach program to provide information on the San Joaquin NWR, San Luis NWR Complex, National Wildlife Refuge System and the U.S. Fish and Wildlife Service.

Narrative: An outreach program is a key component in helping the public become aware of the Refuge, its resources and the public use programs developed for their use and enjoyment. An outreach program would also inform the public about the National Wildlife Refuge System and the Service.

Strategies:
5.8.1 Develop and install entrance and regulatory signs on all public access points to the San Joaquin River NWR.

5.8.2 Work with Caltrans to develop and install directional signs on public roads directing visitors to the San Joaquin River NWR.

5.8.3 Work with the news media to highlight the programs at the San Joaquin River NWR.

5.8.4 Conduct outreach activities regarding the San Joaquin River NWR at local festivals and events.

5.8.5 Develop and produce products to conduct public outreach for the San Joaquin NWR, including a new Complex general brochure, trail guides, posters, fact sheets and other items.

Objective 9. Establish both a volunteer program and Friends group to benefit the San Joaquin River NWR, its resources and its programs.

Narrative: Volunteer programs provide the capacity, at low economic cost, to benefit the Refuge in many different facets. Refuge volunteers can provide valued services in many programmatic areas, including biological monitoring, resource management, administration, nature interpretation, maintenance, and other areas. Volunteers frequently increase the productivity of a station, particularly when it is limited by staffing and funding shortages. A volunteer program also provides avenues for greater community involvement with the Refuge. A Friends group includes community residents who serve as advocates for the Refuge, sharing their enthusiasm about the Refuge with staff and the public. A Friends group typically focuses on conducting or facilitating some large-scale projects at the Refuge each year.

Strategies:
5.9.1 Develop a protocol for a San Joaquin River NWR volunteer program and integrate it with the San Luis NWR Complex's program.

5.9.2 Determine tasks and projects suitable for the volunteer program on a quarterly basis and implement.

5.9.3 Actively recruit volunteers through the media and via Refuge facilities.

5.9.4 Hold a volunteer recognition event annually for the San Luis NWR Complex.

5.9.5 Develop a Refuge Friends group with interested parties for either the San Joaquin River NWR or the San Luis NWR Complex to promote and foster the natural resources of the Refuge and ecoregion. (Same as strategy 4.4.4.)

6 Management Plan Implementation

This CCP will serve as the primary reference document for San Joaquin River NWR planning, operations and management for the next 15 years or until it is formally revised or amended within that period. The Service will implement the CCP with assistance from existing and new partner agencies and organizations and the public. The timing and achievement of the management strategies proposed in this document are contingent upon a variety of factors, including:

- Funding & Staffing
- Step Down Plans
- Compliance Requirements
- Adaptive Management
- Plan Amendment and Revision

Each of these factors is briefly discussed as it applies to the CCP.

Funding & Staffing

The funding required to operate any national wildlife refuge includes initial capital outlay for equipment, facilities, labor and other expenditures, as well as annual, ongoing costs for staff, contracts, supplies, management, maintenance and other recurring expenses (See Table 2: Estimated Initial Capital Outlay to Implement the CCP). Initial expenditures for the Refuge as described in the CCP would cost approximately eight million dollars. Not all of these capital expenditures would accrue during the first year of implementation. For example, habitat development and research would be implemented over the entire length of the plan and select equipment, vehicles and staff may be borrowed or shared from other refuge units of the San Luis NWR Complex. The largest costs for this initial outlay are for habitat restoration and implementation of a public use program. Funding for many of these individual projects will be sought through grants and cooperative partnerships.

At full staffing, personnel dedicated to the Refuge would include a refuge manager, maintenance worker, tractor operator and wildlife biologist. A new public use specialist would be shared with the other units comprising the San Luis NWR Complex. The other staff positions of the Complex are also shared among the different refuge units. Annual contracts or cooperative agreements will be issued for additional law enforcement, fire protection, invasive pest control and other activities as needed. These recurring costs are expected to annually total over half a million dollars (See Table 3: Estimated Annual Cost to Implement the CCP).

Step-Down Management Plans

Some projects or types of projects require more in-depth planning than the CCP process is designed to provide. For these projects, the Service prepares step-down management plans. In essence, step-down management plans provide the additional details necessary to implement management strategies identified in a CCP (See Appendix G: Step-Down Plans).

The National Wildlife Refuge System Manual lists more than 25 Step-Down Management Plans that might be needed at a refuge. These step-down management plans are typically revised at a more frequent interval than a CCP.

Table 2. Estimated Initial Capital Outlay to Implement the CCP

Expenditure	Unit Cost	Unit	Quantity	Total Cost
Office Rehabilitation	$50,000	ea	1	$50,000
Maintenance Shop Construction	$250,000	ea	1	$250,000
Parking Lot	$5,000	ea	3	$15,000
Replace Fencing	$10,000	l.m.	2	$20,000
Replace Gates	$1,000	ea	7	$7,000
Install Automatic Entrance Gate	$10,000	ea	1	$10,000
Erosion Control Materials/Supplies	$10,000	NA	1	$10,000
Habitat Restoration (Upland & Wetland)	$6,000,000	NA	NA	$6,000,000
Brush Rabbit Habitat Restoration	$40,000	NA	NA	$40,000
Lift Pump Rehabilitation & Fish Screens	$100,000	ea	3	$300,000
Pasture Rehabilitation	$200	ac	150	$30,000
Refuge GIS Capability	$30,000	NA	NA	$30,000
Public Tour Route and/or Trails	$250,000	NA	NA	$250,000
Photography Blinds	$12,000	ea	2	$24,000
Public Restrooms	$20,000	ea	2	$40,000
Information Kiosks & Display Panels	$50,000	ea	3	$150,000
Boundary Posting	$30,000	NA	NA	$30,000
Refuge and Regulatory Signs	$3,000	ea	6	$18,000
Boat Launch Facilities	$25,000	ea	2	$50,000
Structure Removal	$20,000	ea	10	$200,000
Recreational Hunt Infrastructure	$10,000	ea	1	$10,000
Recreational Fishing Infrastructure	$40,000	ea	2	$80,000
Concrete Removal	$100,000	NA	NA	$100,000
Dairy Waste Lagoon Cleanup	$35,000	ea	1	$35,000
Tractor	$150,000	ea	1	$150,000
Tractor Implements	$8,000	ea	3	$24,000
All Terrain Vehicle	$6,000	ea	1	$6,000
Misc. Fire Equipment	$10,000	NA	NA	$10,000
Security Alarms for Buildings	$1,500	ea	3	$4,500
Maintenance Equipment	misc	misc	misc	$10,000
Environmental Education Equipment	misc	misc	misc	$10,000
Grand Total:				**$7,963,500**

Table 3. Estimated Annual Cost to Implement the CCP

Expenditure	Unit Cost	Unit	Quantity	Total Cost
Salaries and Benefits				
Complex Project Leader—GS 14	$109,040	ea	0.2	$21,808
Deputy Complex Project Leader—GS 13	$92,270	ea	0.2	$18,454
Refuge Manager—GS 12	$83,000	ea	1.0	$83,000
Complex Admin. Assistant—GS 9	$50,164	ea	0.2	$10,032
Complex Budget Technician—GS 6	$34,070	ea	0.2	$6,814
Engineering Equipment Operator—WG 9	$61,100	ea	1.0	$61,100
Tractor Operator—WG 6	$57,200	ea	1.0	$57,200
Complex Supervisory Wildlife Biol.—GS 12	$83,000	ea	0.2	$16,600
Complex Wildlife Biologist—GS 11	$60,696	ea	0.2	$12,139
Complex Wildlife Biologsit—GS 11	$60,696	ea	0.2	$12,139
Complex Wildlife Biologist—GS 9	$50,164	ea	0.2	$10,032
Refuge Wildlife Biologist—GS 9	$50,164	ea	1.0	$50,164
Complex Public Use Specialist—GS 12	$83,000	ea	0.2	$16,600
Complex Public Use Specialist—GS 9	$50,164	ea	0.3	$15,049
Complex Park Ranger—GS 9	$50,164	ea	0.2	$10,032
Complex Fire Mgmt. Officer—GS 11	$60,696	ea	0.2	$12,139
Complex Fire Specialist—GS 9	$50,164	ea	0.2	$10,032
Complex Lead Forest Tech—GS 8	$45,417	ea	0.2	$9,083
Complex Perm. Seas. Forest Tech—GS6	$34,070	ea	0.1	$3,407
Complex Perm. Seas. Forest Tech—GS5	$33,107	ea	0.1	$3,311
Complex Perm. Seas. Forest Tech—GS5	$33,107	ea	0.1	$3,311
Complex Temp. Seas. Forest Tech—GS5	$25,467	ea	0.1	$2,547
Complex Temp. Seas. Forest Tech—GS4	$22,762	ea	0.1	$2,276
Complex Temp. Seas. Forest Tech—GS3	$20,277	ea	0.1	$2,027
Maintenance	$50,000	ea	1.0	$50,000
Invasive Weed Program	$20,000	ea	1.0	$20,000
Water/Pumping Costs	$25,000	ea	1.0	$25,000
Riparian Brush Rabbit Monitoring	$10,000	ea	1.0	$10,000
Water Quality Monitoring	$10,000	ea	1.0	$10,000
Travel/Training	$5,000	NA	1.0	$5,000
Supplies	$25,000	ea	1.0	$25,000
Printing	$5,000	ea	1.0	$5,000
Pump-out for restroom	$5,000	ea	4.0	$20,000
Grand Total:				**$619,296**

*Current or anticipated step-down
plans for the San Joaquin River NWR
include:*

Plans that are current and up-to-date:
■ Fire Management Plan (2001)
■ Spill Response Plan (2003)
■ Safety Management Plan (2000)
■ Continuity of Operations Plan (1999)

Plans that exist but need to be updated:
■ Disease Management Plan (1983)
■ Emergency Management Plan (1993)

Plans that need to be initiated:
■ Water Management Plan
■ Law Enforcement Plan
■ Public Use Management Plan
■ Upland Management Plan
■ Fisheries Management Plan
■ Invasive Exotic Plant Control Plan

Compliance Requirements

This CCP was developed to comply
with all applicable Federal laws,
executive orders, and legislative acts.
Some activities, particularly those that
involve revising an existing step-down
management plan or preparing a new
one, will need to comply with additional
laws or regulations besides NEPA and the
National Wildlife Refuge Improvement
Act. In addition to these acts, full
implementation of all components of this
CCP requires compliance with other laws
and mandates (See Appendix J: Relevant
Federal Laws and Mandates).

Adaptive Management & Monitoring

Evaluation

Adaptive management is the process
of implementing policy decisions as
scientifically driven experiments that
test predictions and assumptions about
management plans, using the resulting
information to improve the plans.
Management direction is periodically
evaluated via a system of applying several
options, monitoring the objectives, and
adapting original strategies to reach
desired objectives. Habitat, wildlife

and public use management techniques
and specific objectives will be regularly
evaluated as results of a monitoring
program and other new technology and
information become available. These
periodic evaluations would be used over
time to adapt both the management
objectives and strategies to better achieve
management goals. Such a system
embraces uncertainty, reduces option
foreclosure, and provides new information
for future decision-making while allowing
resource use. At a minimum, each year
a checklist of the goals, objectives and
management strategies of this CCP will
be completed to assist in tracking and
evaluating progress (Appendix P).

Monitoring

Monitoring is an essential component
of the CCP. Monitoring strategies have
been integrated into many of this plan's
goals and objectives. Specific details,
including monitoring strategies, methods,
techniques and locations, will be outlined
in a step-down Monitoring Plan. In this
CCP, habitat monitoring receives an
important emphasis.

All habitat management activities will be
monitored to assess whether the desired
effects on wildlife and habitat components
have been achieved. Baseline surveys
will be conducted for wildlife species for
which existing or historical numbers and
occurrences are not well known. Studies
will also monitor wildlife responses to
increased public use of the Refuge for
fishing, hunting, wildlife observation and
environmental education.

Monitoring will be designed and developed
in cooperation with universities and
non-governmental organizations to the
greatest extent possible. Applied research
can provide insight into ecological
questions concerning habitat, wildlife and
public use management. Refuge staff
would work with researchers to ensure
that investigations are applicable and
compatible with Refuge objectives.

Maintaining and restoring habitat quality and quantity are a major means of accomplishing Refuge goals and objectives. Monitoring would focus on measuring vegetative diversity and abundance, water quality and quantity and wildlife response to management practices. Baseline surveys would be established for other species for which existing or historical numbers are not established.

Progress toward Refuge goals and objectives will be evaluated based on the results of this station's monitoring activities.

Plan Amendment and Revision

This CCP is intended to evolve as the Refuge changes, and the Improvement Act specifically requires formal revision and updating of CCPs at least every 15 years. The formal revision process would follow the same steps as the CCP creation process. In the meantime, the Service would be reviewing and updating this CCP periodically based on the results of its adaptive management program. This

CCP would also be informally reviewed by Refuge staff while preparing annual work plans and updating Refuge databases. It may also be reviewed during routine inspections or programmatic evaluations. Results of any or all of these reviews may indicate a need to modify the plan.

The goals described in this CCP would not change until they are reevaluated as part of the formal CCP revision process. However, the objectives and strategies may be revised to better address changing circumstances or to take advantage of increased knowledge of the resources at the Refuge. If changes are required, the level of public involvement and associated NEPA documentation would be determined by the Refuge Manager.

Refuge objectives and strategies are intended to be attained over the next 15 years. Management activities would be phased in over time and implementation is contingent upon and subject to results of monitoring and evaluation, funding levels and staffing.

www.ingramcontent.com/pod-product-compliance
Lightning Source LLC
Chambersburg PA
CBHW081228280526
45787CB00006B/2573